Mountain bike racing

Tim Gould and Simon Burney

A & C Black • London

Published by A & C Black (Publishers)
Ltd, 35 Bedford Row, London WC1R
4JH

First edition 1992
Revised paperback edition 1996

ISBN 0 7136 4439 7

A CIP catalogue record for this book
is available from the British Library.

Printed and bound in Hong Kong by
Colorcraft

Acknowledgements

The author and publishers are grateful to
the following for supplying photographs
to illustrate the text:

Steve Behr of Stockfile, for the
photographs on pages 136 and 138

Malcolm Fearon for the photographs on
pages 21, 22, 23, 25, 28, 29 (4), 30 (4),
33, 37 (2), 39 (top and bottom), 44 (2)
and 47

KL Photographers, York, for the
photographs on page 106

Willie Mathews, for the photographs on
pages 18, 20, 35, 36, 54, 60, 92 (left),
128 and 131

Huw Williams, for the photographs on
pages 26, 27, 39, 41 (top), 53, 65, 71,
89, 90, 107 (right), 108, 116, 125, 132
and 134

All other photography, including the
cover pictures by Stewart Clarke

We should also like to acknowledge the
help of Peter Keen and Roger
Palfreeman with the text on the four
training levels; the IMBA for permission
to reproduce the *Rules of the Trail*; Karin
Zeitvogel and Tim Clifford for their help
with the world championship results; and
Guy Andrews for his help with the text

cover photographs
front: John Tomac on his way to gold in
the 1991 World Championship cross-
country

back: the breathtaking scenery of
Chateau d'Oex in Switzerland, host to
the penultimate round of the 1991
Grundig World Cup Series

frontispiece: Tom Rogers giving a fine
display of controlled falling in the 1990
World Championship downhill at
Durango

Contents

1 Introduction

What is mountain bike racing?

As recently as the early 1980s, if you had gone into a bike shop and asked to look at a mountain bike, you would have come away disappointed! The mountain bike was still being hatched such a short time ago, and yet now you can't fail to see them being ridden in towns and cities, parks and trails. This proves that the mountain bike was the success story of the eighties not only for the cycle industry, but for the leisure industry as a whole, as a new generation of people was introduced to the pleasures of cycling. Now, in the nineties, mountain bike racing is the fastest growing form of cycle sport, and one of the most popular.

To most people back then, cycling conjured up images of the heavy roadster with a basket on the front, a group of head-down, bottom up fanatics tearing along on thin tyres with even thinner saddles, or – horror of horrors –

Even in city parks mountain bike racing proves popular. This circuit at Eastway, London, attracts hundreds of racers

the static exercise bike bought during a particularly 'fat' moment to shed that flab.

Mountain bikes changed the whole image of cycling. Suddenly it was enjoyable, comfortable and stylish to go out for a ride. Smaller wheels, comfortable seats, gears that were easy to work, and no more walking up hills!

And, of course, when a leisure activity becomes popular, it's only human nature for it to become competitive; and so mountain bike racing began. At first the rules were simple: there weren't any! Groups of friends would see who could ride the fastest, mainly downhill. But word soon got out, the cycle industry caught on, and suddenly everybody wanted a go! Organisations of mountain bikers were formed, first in the USA then in Europe. Basic guidelines were set out, and rules kept to a minimum.

The basic form of racing is the cross-country event, held off-road on a circuit varying in length from around 4 miles (7km) to as much as 20 miles (35km). Riders face whatever nature cares to offer them, from the wilds of mountainous

terrain to the grassy slopes of town parks. All-terrain bikes go wherever course designers decide a challenge can be met.

Race times vary according to ability: from around one hour for novice classes to three hours or more for the pros – yes, professional mountain bike racers do exist! At the elite end of the sport the professional class is thriving, with sponsorship and endorsements coming from a rejuvenated cycle industry as well as from large multinational companies eager to take advantage of the media coverage attracted to the sport.

Accepted in 1990 by the world governing body of cycling, mountain biking now boasts not one World Championship event but two! The coveted rainbow jersey is also awarded for the downhill race as well as for the cross-country. The downhill is quite simply a time-trial event to find the fastest person down a mountain, and downhill specialists have to be fearless as well as superb bike handlers.

But we have to go back to the mid-seventies and to Marin County, California, to see how it all began...

A brief history of mountain bike racing

It was all started by a group of guys seeing who could go downhill fastest on their 'clunkers' – home-made bikes with parts taken from tandems and motorbikes. These same guys are now household names in mountain bike circles. Gary Fisher, Tom Ritchey, Joe Breeze, Charlie Kelly and Charlie Cunningham started out bodging bikes from anything they could find and trying to keep them together for long enough to descend the famous Repack downhill race, run as a time trial down a dirt road in Marin County, California.

Mountain bikes were developed along these lines by the likes of Fisher and Ritchey, and commercial production eventually started in the late seventies, with the first mass-produced model sourced from the Far East by Mike Sinyard of Specialized in the early eighties.

It was then, with mass-produced mountain bikes available in bike shops, that racing started to take off and to become more organised, and the need for a governing body to document rules and to provide liability insurance was met when the US National Off-Road Bicycle Association (NORBA) was formed in 1983.

Rules were kept to a minimum: it was because road racing was so rule-bound that people were driven to find an alternative form of cycle sport, where it didn't matter if you didn't have a licence and you rode in cut-off jeans, and it has been this easy-going attitude to racing that has attracted such a large following in such a small space of time. Even now you can go into a bike shop on a Saturday, buy a bike and a helmet, and be on the start line on Sunday. This is not possible in any other form of cycle sport.

The first NORBA-sanctioned National Mountain Bike Championships were held in 1983, and news soon travelled to Europe, where similar bodies started springing up to control and sanction racing in each country.

The first World Championships were held in 1987. There were in fact two, one at Mammoth, California, and one at Villard-des-Lans in the French Alps, and this was to be the story for the next two years, until the UCI took control via its affiliated national bodies such as the BCF in Britain and USCF in America. The stage was then set for worldwide agreement on rules, regulations and world championships in mountain biking, which all happened in Purgatory, Colorado, in 1990 at the first unified World Championships.

But what of the pioneers?
Happily, they are still around and contributing more than ever to the sport they started. Sinyard, Fisher and Ritchey made the transition from enthusiasts to businessmen, and their innovations in equipment lead the way in the fastest-moving area of cycle sales. However, they still continue to be involved in racing: Tom Ritchey sponsors one of the most successful race teams in the world, on a par with the dominant Specialized team, while Gary Fisher is still not ready to hang up his wheels and competed in the veteran class at the 1990 and 1991 world championships.

And the future? Well, it looks rosy. The sceptics who thought the whole thing was a craze which would fizzle out like BMX, have been proved wrong. Sales show signs of stabilising, races are becoming established, and the personalities are developing.

Above all, mountain bike racing has come through the opening chapter of its life with the deserved image of a fun, healthy, accessible pastime: long may you enjoy it!

How the sport is run

What of the rules? Even with the introduction of high-level racing and governing bodies, the rule book remains thin. There are two fundamental rules. First, bikes must have wheels no larger than 26 inches, with tyres no thinner than 1.5 inches, two brakes and plugged handlebars. Second – and this is equally strictly adhered to – the rider must be self-sufficient, with no outside

assistance or technical support in the event of punctures or breakages. This is the rule that cyclo-cross riders cannot come to terms with, being used to changing bikes every lap and having mechanics clean and mend their bikes. However, it is the spirit of mountain biking that everybody has the same chance, and the rider with the most bikes, or the one who punctures just by a technical support area, has no advantage. Everyone carries spare inner tubes and tyre levers, and the race is won by the rider who is not only the fittest but the best able to keep his bike out of trouble.

Runners, cyclists and horses battle it out in the Man v Horse race, one of the British classics

For the detailed rules applicable to your country, you need to contact your governing body, as categories of riders, licence requirements and age groups can vary slightly from country to country.

The general riding rules, however, are universal, and cover such areas as safety, trespass and rights of way. Below are listed the Off-road Code and the International Mountain Bike Association Rules of the Trail. They aren't trying to curtail your fun, just giving good advice for the users of the great outdoors, so abide by them at all times!

The Off-road Code

- Only ride where you know you have a legal right to do so.
- Always give way to horses and to pedestrians.
- Avoid animals and crops. In some circumstances this may not be possible, in which case contact should be kept to a minimum.
- Take all litter with you.
- Leave all gates as found.
- Keep the noise down.
- Don't get annoyed with anyone; it never solves any problems.
- Always try to be self-sufficient, for yourself and your bike.
- Never create a fire hazard.
- Avoid bunching up with other riders and obstructing a trail.
- Always tell someone where you are going, and give an estimated time of arrival.
- Smile a lot.

IMBA Rules of the Trail

Thousands of miles of dirt trails have been closed to mountain bikers because of the irresponsible riding habits of a few riders. Do your part to maintain trail access by observing the following rules of the trail, which originated in the US but have been adopted generally:

1 Ride on open trails only. Respect trail and road closures (ask if not sure), avoid possible trespass on private land, and obtain permits and authorisation as may be required. Federal and State wilderness areas are closed to cycling. Additional trails may be closed because of sensitive environmental concerns or conflicts with other users. Your riding example will determine what is closed to all cyclists!

2 Leave no trace. Be sensitive to the dirt beneath you. Even on open trails, you should not ride under conditions where you will leave evidence of your passing, such as on certain soil after rain. Observe the different types of soils and trail construction; practise low-impact cycling. This also means staying on the trail and not creating any new ones. Be sure to pack out at least as much as you pack in.

3 Control your bicycle! Inattention for even a second can cause disaster. Excessive speed maims and threatens people; there is no excuse for it!

4 Always yield trail. Make known your approach well in advance. A friendly greeting (or bell) is considerate and works well; startling someone may cause loss of trail access. Show your respect when passing others by slowing to a walk or even stopping. Anticipate that other trail users may be around corners or in blind spots.

5 Never spook animals. All animals are startled by an unannounced approach, a sudden movement, or a loud noise. This can be dangerous for you, others, and the animals. Give animals extra room and time to adjust to you. In passing, use special care and follow the directions of horseback riders (if uncertain). Running cattle and disturbing wild animals is a serious offence. Leave gates as you found them, or as marked.

6 Plan ahead. Know your equipment, your ability, and the area in which you are riding and prepare accordingly. Be self-sufficient at all times, keep your machine in good repair, and carry necessary supplies for changes in weather or other conditions. A well-executed trip is a satisfaction to you and not a burden or offence to others. Keep trails open by setting an example of responsible cycling for all mountain bicyclists.

2 Racing for beginners

There are different categories of competitors based on ability, age and sex, to enable everybody to compete against people of a similar standard. Beginners start in a category called 'novice' or 'fun/weekender'. You are not forced to move up to the next category, but if you regularly win in a particular category then you will probably be advised to move up.

The bike

There are very few rules concerning the bike. As we have seen, wheels must have a maximum diameter of 26 inches and tyres a minimum width of 1.5 inches. This means that road bike wheels are not allowed. Most events have a machine examination. This is a brief safety check on the wheels, brakes and gears to stop you from injuring yourself or anybody else through bad maintenance of your bike. After successful completion of this check you will be issued with your race number. Because only one bike per competitor is allowed, one of the numbers is usually attached

You are never too young to start!

to the bike to show that it is the same bike that started and finished the race.

Don't be afraid that your bike may not be good enough to race on. Sure, the professionals race on very expensive machines, but they didn't start off on bikes like that, they started on much more humble machines and upgraded as their ability and enthusiasm grew. The important thing is that your bike

fits you well, in other words that the saddle and handlebar stem are adjusted to your particular requirements. Also, as mountain bike racing requires you to be self-sufficient, the bike needs to be in first-class mechanical order.

The most important part of the bike is the frame. It's always best to buy the highest-quality frame you can afford. The other parts of the bike will get worn more quickly and so

Young and old, fit or not, anyone can race a mountain bike

will require replacing whether they are expensive or not. After the frame the next most important parts are the wheels. If you're spending money on equipment it is a good plan to have a pair of wheels just for racing and to keep your original wheels for training. Mountain bike racing is very easy to get started in compared with other branches of cycle sport, and has consequently attracted many people new to cycle racing. This is because as long as you've got a mountain bike and shell helmet you can turn up at a race and take part. Other branches of cycle sport require you to have a licence and clothing conforming to regulations.

For the beginner in mountain biking this is not necessary; you can turn up in any clothes you want, and you don't need a licence.

Although it is not compulsory to join a cycling or mountain-biking club, it is a very good idea. Your local mountain bike shop will advise you of any clubs in the area. The club members will help you, and maybe even give you a lift to some races.

If you intend competing in races in other countries then you will need a racing licence from your national mountain bike governing body. You will also need a licence when you progress from the novice category.

Some basic information to put you in the picture is given below; you will find more detail in the later chapters.

Finding a race

Forthcoming races are listed in the 'calendar of events' sections of specialist mountain bike magazines such as *Mountain Biker,*

Mountain Biking UK and *Mountainbike Action.* For your first race it would be a good idea to enter one that's in your locality, and such races will probably be advertised in your local bike shop. Most major events need to be entered in advance by sending your entry fee and completed entry form to the event organiser. An accepted entry ensures that you will get a race. A lot of events are over-subscribed, so it is a good idea to enter early, as allocation is normally on a first-come-first-served basis.

You will need a water-bottle cage and bottle, as most races are over an hour in duration. Because of the self-sufficiency rule you'll need the ability to make repairs and take enough spares to solve foreseeable problems. This means taking a spare inner tube, tyre levers, chain-

rivet extractor and a couple of Allen keys in an under-saddle bag.

Clothing

How many clothes you need obviously depends on the conditions. For most events you will be able to race in just shorts, under-jersey and short-sleeved racing top. If the course has water crossings or long descents you'll need some warming embrocation on your legs.

There are many brands of mountain bike shoe or boot on the market, and a well-fitting pair of these will aid your cycling efficiency much more than a pair of sunglasses!

For a full discussion of mountain bike clothing and footwear, see chapter 5.

3 The racing season

Mountain bike racing is primarily a summer sport, although occasional winter races are staged if you feel like keeping your hand in during the off season.

Most major races start in April, and from then on the schedule is hectic, until the World Championships bring the season to a close at the end of September or early October.

The World Cup series starts in Europe for three rounds in April and May; then the Americans take over for an eight-week period from June onwards, when they also have the majority of the NORBA series races. The circus travels back to Europe for the final races in August and September, when the European Championships and finals of most national series take place. Then it's the big one – the World Championships, which alternate annually between the USA and Europe, with Australia set to join the scene in 1996.

As you can see internationally there is not much time to spare for a rest, and domestically the calendar is no clearer – if you are prepared to

Big time: the start of a World Championship general competitors' race

travel you can find a race every weekend from March until the end of September.

In the big series, consistency is the key. Maintaining your standard for six months requires good planning and not doing too much too soon. Don't be like the many riders who train like crazy all winter, win by minutes in March and April, and then disappear from all the results when the racing hots up.

Consistency is vital, but so is the ability to peak for the championship races. Over a series of six or eight rounds you can have a couple of off days and still come away with a high overall placing, especially if the five best results out of eight count, for example: but for championship races – world, European or national – you have just one shot at it, and if you have a bad day, you don't get a second chance. Mentally, championship races are the toughest, and although some people think that a true world champion should come from a season-long series of races to prove that he or she is the best on all courses everywhere, the one-day World Championship race will always have a worthy winner

who shows that preparation and mental toughness count.

Many European mountain bike racers come from a road-racing and cyclo-cross background and still involve themselves with these branches of the sport. This gives them an even busier year, with cyclo-cross running from October to the end of February, and the road-racing in parallel with the mountain bike season. In the States, cyclo-cross is on a much smaller scale, with only a handful of races each winter, and a lot of riders take this winter break as the opportunity to practise other sports – skiing being the most popular. Again, road riders in the states have also made the cross over with success and carry on mixing the two; John Tomac did it the other way and went from mountain bike to road racing. For the majority of riders, however, racing off-road comes first and they stick to what they know!

If you are just stepping out in the world of mountain bike racing, it is important not to limit yourself just to this one type of cycle racing, especially if you are young: try them all – road, criteriums, 'cross, even track if it is accessible. Not only will they make you a better off-road rider, but you might find success at these other branches as well. Tomac, Frischknecht, Kluge and Grewal, some of the world's leading mountain bike racers, have all represented their countries at road, cyclo-cross or track.

Off-road racing is hard, and many of the qualities required to do it well are the same as those for racing on the road. Strength is a prime requirement for both, and stamina from long road races is of great value when the going gets tough after a couple of hours on your mountain bike.

Cyclo-cross is basically an hour-long intensive effort, ridden on a smaller circuit on what are basically road bikes with knobbly tyres and slight changes to brakes and gearing. Such is the effort involved, both on the bike and running with it over the hardest parts of the course, that it has been 'cross riders who have made the biggest impact on mountain bike races in recent years. With the exception of Mike Kloser and John Tomac, virtually no big race in Europe has been won by a rider without a 'cross background; in fact specialist European mountain bikers are hard to find – all of them can turn their hands to anything.

Stateside the story is different. 'Cross is a bit of a mystery to all but a few who have tried it in Europe, such as Don Myrah, the 1989 World Champion, who has lived and raced in Switzerland, the home of European cyclo-cross. The likes of Ned Overend, John Tomac and Greg Herbold have given it a miss and still perform admirably without it.

Our advice is this: if you live in an area that has a good calendar of 'cross and road racing, take part, as it can only do you good. But if you are in an area without a strong following, don't worry – if Ned can do it, so can you with the right training!

The link with traditional cycling is the basic difference between the pros in Europe and those in America.

In Europe cycling is everything: plenty of races to ride on- or off-road, twelve months a year, based on a calendar that stretches back over the years. If there is no mountain bike race, the top guys eagerly seek out a road race, and spend the winter on the 'cross circuit. In Britain, Belgium and Holland midweek criteriums on tight city-centre circuits provide the chance to race two or three times a week, and are excellent training. The demands of sponsors are instrumental in forcing their riders to race frequently, gaining as much exposure as possible.

In America the scene is different. Fewer races, but with a higher profile, fill only a five-month season, and the winter is spent following other activities. Sponsors stick to either road or mountain bikes, and riders rarely ride both for the same sponsor, so there is less pressure to race constantly.

Compare the competition programmes of Ned Overend and Tim Gould. Ned probably rides a maximum of 30 races a year, all mountain bike. Tim last year rode 25 mountain bike races, 45 road and criterium races and 20 cyclo-crosses, totalling 90 races. You cannot say one is right and one wrong, it is simply the way the two countries operate. America is so large that far more time is spent travelling to and from races, and you are hardly likely to ride an hour-long criterium in Michigan if you live in San Francisco and need to catch a plane to get there! Europe, on the other hand, has plenty nearby – if you want to ride a criterium in Belgium, for instance, you could race every day within 40 miles of Ghent!

'He sure goes fast for a skinny guy' John Tomac on Tim Gould

4 Equipment

Modern mountain bikes and equipment have evolved so quickly since the mid-eighties that there is no norm. Because ideas are changing so fast, it is all too easy to become caught up in keeping up with current trends and designs. Don't forget the main criterion for choosing either a complete bike or components to build a bike for mountain bike racing, and that is to be able to perform to the best of your physical ability on an efficient, reliable machine.

It is a hard task to evaluate the endless stream of new components, all claiming to be the lightest/fastest/most radical yet, and a glance through any mountain bike magazine is enough to confuse even the most technical wizards. As you become more experienced as a racer you will come to realise what extras you really need, and which you can save for the bike to cruise around posing on!

Specialist downhill races require specialist equipment, and Mammoth's 'Kamikaze' merits 60 x 12 gearing. Not many pairs of legs could pedal a gear that size, but John Tomac isn't just any pair of legs . . .

Don't be fooled into thinking that most expensive is best when shopping around for your equipment. With exotic materials being used for everything from frames and forks to seat pins and bottle cages, the prices can vary enormously; but higher prices don't always result in better performance, so be wary. It is far more important to make sure the bike fits the rider and to maintain the equipment used. In mountain bike racing, more than any other type of cycle racing, the bike takes an absolute hammering and must be looked after thoroughly if it is to get you through a race.

Over the next few sections we will discuss the parts that make up the bike in more detail, outlining what is currently available and the various pros and cons of each alternative.

The frame

The heart of the bike is the frame, and this, more than any other item, must be correct for you. The material the frame is made from and the size and design of the frame all affect the bike's performance, and no matter what components are used, if the frame is wrong, the bike is wrong!

So let us start with the materials frames can be made from.

Frame materials

Steel

Steel, long the traditional material for making road bikes, is still popular for mountain bikes. Because of the range of qualities of steel, it can be used on everything from the cheapest bike to the hand-built superlight racing machine. With a large selection to choose from, you are bound to be able to find a steel frame within your price range. It also offers the advantage of a made-to-measure frame, which means that you can order a frame to your specification, with features that may not be available on a stock frame.

Steel has the advantage of being easy to repair, and all round is the least expensive material to build in.

The weight of the frame decreases as the tubing wall thickness is reduced, but to reduce wall thickness overall weakens the frame. To overcome this, tubing manufacturers 'butt' the tubes

making them thicker at the ends where they are joined and where building and riding stresses are greatest, and thinner in the middle of the tubes where frames rarely fail.

Tom Ritchey, frame builder to a number of the world's leading riders, has developed the lightest available steel tube sets in conjunction with Tange, by producing a tube with a shorter, thicker butt at the ends which can withstand the heat of TIG welding during the building process, but which allows a much longer thin area along the tube, reducing weight significantly.

Frames built from tubing of this quality give a very responsive ride but unfortunately have quite a limited life – a heavy season of racing is usually enough to mean replacement at the end of the year and demotion to training bike status!

Another way of lightening steel frames is to increase the size! This sounds paradoxical, but the theory behind oversize tubing is that as you increase the diameter of the tube, its strength increases, thereby allowing you to reduce the wall thickness and weight. This is fine in principle, but causes problems with fitting conventional

Aluminum oversize frames such as the Klein, seen here being ridden by Cindy Devine, have the advantage of light weight and strength

Another example of using oversized aluminium tubing for frame design is this American Trimble

mechanisms which are sized for road-diameter tubing. Most manufacturers now offer several sizes of components to cope with the varied sizes of frame tubing. Headset diameters are a hot issue. The standard sizes are 1inch or 1¹/₈inch, but most are 1¹/₈inch giving a thicker, stronger headtube and bigger welding surfaces for attaching frame

tubes, especially important for aluminium bikes. It's more popular with mass manufacturers. Many custom steel builders prefer the 1inch headtube and use reinforcing fillets on the down tube to beef up the joints for suspension.

Aluminium

From the vast array of materials available to use for frame construction, aluminium still proves to be the most popular. It has a much lower density than

steel, so for the same weight a much stronger frame can be built – or, by reducing the strength to that of a light steel frame, a good saving in weight can be made.

Aluminium frames in conventional tubing diameters similar to those of road bikes have the advantage that they can be built with lugs which are threaded, and screwed and glued to the tube. However, the wall thickness of standard diameter tubes has to be a lot greater to make the frame rigid so to increase the rigidity and reduce the weight, most manufacturers use oversize tubing.

The major disadvantage of aluminium is that it is hard to repair in case of a breakage, and if there are any aluminium threads on the frame, more care is needed to prevent them from seizing or stripping.

Carbon fibre

Carbon fibre has excellent properties for frame building: it's light, strong, rigid, and is getting easier to manufacture so it's also cheaper. In recent years the use of carbon fibre for mountain bikes has been mostly for reinforcement of components like suspension where extra strength is needed. A carbon frame can offer a solid ride, although its characteristics are not good if comfort is a priority.

The main advantage of using carbon fibre is in the number of ways the frame can be constructed. The carbon layers can be wrapped around a mould, so that by adding layers in certain areas and in certain directions, strength can be improved as required.

The joints are the weak spots on a carbon-fibre frame. If this problem can be overcome by one-piece moulding, all well and good; if not, lugs are required, and these can provide opportunities for frame failure.

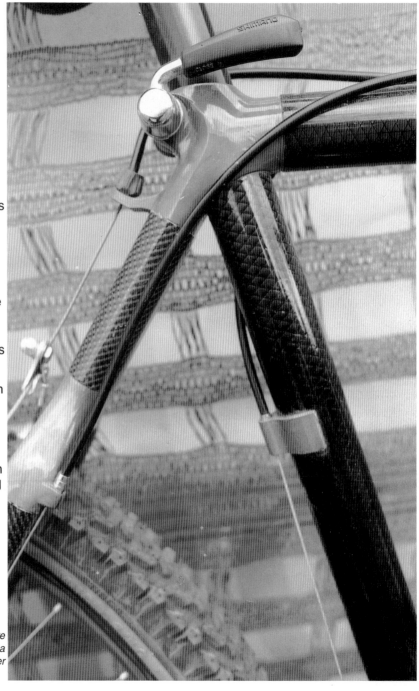

Here carbon/Kevlar tubes are neatly bonded to a lug to produce a clean-looking seat cluster

Titanium

Titanium is the ultimate material for for frame construction: very light, very strong and durable, but incredibly expensive. If money is no object go for it!

Variables

The frame is just the starting point of a good MTB, and mixing frame materials is a frame builder's delight. They can turn tube sets upside down, mix and match steels, and create your ideal bike for you. Aluminium rear suspension units can be bolted onto a custom frame; the possibilities are endless.

Forks are now the key to a good bike, and the choice of material, suspension or not, makes all the difference. Builders incorporate these options into the design – so the choice is yours, whatever the conditions.

Frame design

The million-dollar question is: what is the best frame design?

Every frame builder and every rider has an opinion on the 'ultimate' design of a mountain bike frame. The important point to bear in mind is that the bike must fit you, must be comfortable and suitable for the purpose intended. We could fill a book with the various design features available on a frame, but instead we prefer to tell you what has worked for us and why.

Some frame designers will try anything! This Sling Shot has a tensioned cable in place of the traditional downtube

The frame that Tim rides

The most practical shape for a mountain bike (or any bike really) is a diamond pattern, similar to that of a road bike. This means you can shoulder the bike cyclo-cross style for running sections, which is especially important in muddy British conditions. It's also the strongest configuration, getting the most from the materials to give a fast, responsive ride. Frame design has changed due to the popularity of suspension, and this affects the angles of the frame tubes as suspension puts the front end up a bit. Non-suspension bikes now have longer forks to allow for suspension to be fitted.

A headtube angle of 71° and a seat angle somewhere between 72° and 74° are good guidlines, but opinion varies according to fashion, frame materials and your body shape.

Sloping toptubes are becoming the norm with suspension corrected bikes. They have a higher front end and require the top tube to slope backwards to give stand-over height, so jumping on and off is less of a problem. It also means a

Head angle	71°
Seat angle	74°
Chainstays	16.9in (42.9cm)
Fork rake	1.8in (4.6cm)
Bottom bracket	
(with 2in tyre)	11.5 (29.2cm)
Wheelbase	42.4in (107.7cm)

The longer than average toptube on Tim's frame is designed to accommodate his relatively long back and short legs

tighter, stiffer back end that kicks on climbs and reacts well on fast, single track.

Chainstays must be wide enough at the front to give adequate clearance for a 2.1inch tyre and not to get clogged up if conditions are muddy. They must not be too short, which can cause a bumpy ride and problems with the chainline: 16.9inch is a good standard length – don't go shorter than 16.5inch unless you intend to use the bike purely for hillclimbs.

Full suspension bikes are becoming popular with cross-country riders. The use of lighter materials means a swing arm back end and shock can be fitted, still keeping the bike's weight to under 26lbs. The advantages on downhill sections are obvious, but climbing can be laborious. Races could

thus be won on downhill ability alone, in which case their popularity will undoubtedly increase.

Bottle-cage bosses should be fitted on the downtube and the seat tube as low as possible. On the seat tube this usually means one boss either side of the front mechanism clamp. Keeping them low keeps the centre of gravity near the bottom bracket, which means you can pick your bike up with the downtube and carry it on your shoulder without fear of snapping the bottle cages.

As for the brazed-on bits to hang brakes, bottles, etc, on, again keep them simple and tidy, and use split cable stops so that you can drop the cables out easily to re-lubricate.

Keep cables short and neat

Brake pivots for cantilevers are standard and should be positioned correctly by the builder.

Route the back brake cable along the top of the tube with a section of bare cable between the stops at the front and back of the top tube, or you can even route the bare cable through an eye brazed onto the seat cluster.

Gear cable is best routed across the toptubes as it allows for easy cable servicing and prevents mud getting into cable outers or collecting under the bottom bracket. It also stops the cables from catching on clothing or trail debris.

Forks

Once upon a time, forks were simply forks! They were made from the same material as the frame, with a rake or curve at the bottom, and they were replaced only when damaged. Nowadays the choice is more varied: steel or aluminium; straight or bent; suspension or not

Let's start with the material they should be made from. Steel is by far the most sensible choice for rigid forks, even with a fancy titanium or carbon-fibre frame.

The revolution in front suspension has produced a wide variety of different types of fork. These are Quasar forks

Steel is resilient enough to absorb large amounts of shock before it reaches the handlebars and your arms, but strong enough always to go back to its original form. It can be made into a responsive fork to cope with any amount of technical downhill or single-track riding.

A recent fashion has been the use of straight forks, claimed to make the bike more responsive. The reason for the curve of the bottom portion of the fork is to absorb shock and give a more comfortable ride, and by varying this curve you determine the handling characteristics of the steering. We believe the cons outweigh the pros of straight forks, so go for the curved variety.

Suspension forks

Suspension forks came originally from motor bikes and until recently were the reserve of downhillers. They were heavy and fairly unreliable, so not much use for cross-country racing. The developments in suspension and materials are constantly changing; they get better all the time. This means that they are a viable and useful alternative to rigid forks, indeed all World Cup and serious amateur racers are now using suspension.

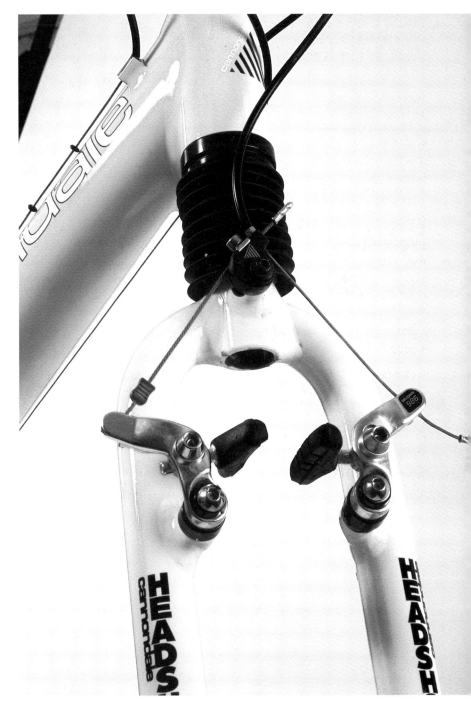

Cannondale are one of the first companies to enclose the suspension unit within the frame's headtube

Essentially there are two types of suspension fork: elastomer, where special density plastic bumpers are the spring; and air/oil, where the air is the spring and the oil provides some dampening to make the recoil of the spring less aggressive over bumps. The downside is that air/oil forks take a lot of servicing and can burst oil seals at inopportune moments or lose air through the valves. With elastomer forks, friction on the seals provides the dampening which is effective but less plush than air/oil.

Thus the new generation forks are a combination of both systems: elastomers for the bounce, with an oil cartridge inside the legs to provide the dampening. These are proving popular with racers. Variations and alterations to accommodate all conditions are possible so you can adjust the forks wherever you're racing.

Market leader Rock Shox

Swiss Cilo design featuring standard steel
forks with suspension unit attached

Italian Marzocchi aluminium forks

Suspenders with disc brake

Manitou forks

Catching up quickly is rear suspension. This is a Cannondale with elevated chainstays

Greg Herbold's Miyata features adapted rear Rock Shox and variable rear geometry. And you thought bikes were simple!

Aerospace air-dampened rear suspension

Pro-flex

Wheels

The most important components of your bike are undoubtedly the wheels. Just as your frame is vital to the comfort of the bike, the wheels need to be built correctly and with the right components to ensure that the transmission runs smoothly, the brakes work well, and effort is not wasted through loose or bent wheels.

Your wheels are made up of four critical things: rims, hubs, spokes and tender loving care! We will look at all four in more detail.

Rims

The trend is for rims to be as narrow as possible, even down to around 20mm, which is the same as a road rim. However, at this width it can be very hard to fit tyres and tubes, so it is wise to choose rims a little wider – 23-25mm is best.

As with all components on a bike, the choice between weight-saving and strength is critical: too light, and the wheel will flex under pressure on a climb and the rim will be more susceptible to denting; too strong, and you will find yourself able to ride down the roughest trail but the wheel will give a 'dead' ride on the flat and the extra weight will have to be dragged back uphill. Don't be tempted to try and save too much weight: you need good, strong, reliable wheels

Eight sprockets will fit! The Campagnolo 8-speed cassette reduces the jumps between sprockets and fits in the same space as a 7-speed.

left: a 1.9in multi-use tyre – ideal if you use your bike on- and off-road
middle: a 1.9in studded tyre – good in the mud or on faster circuits on grassland
right: a 2.1 Megabite – ideal for deep, loose ground and rough , rocky descents

Many new rim designs are now using the 'V' cross-section, which gives good rigidity and reinforces the points where the spokes go through, reducing the need for eyelets for the spoke nipples to sit in, and thus saving a bit more weight.

Deep section rims are being developed for extra strength and mud-cutting stability; they also look pretty good. But a rim is only as good as the builder who puts the wheel together, so consult a professional about what's going to do the best job for your type of riding.

Hubs

Almost universally used nowadays

are the cassette-type hubs, where the freewheel body is part of the hub, and the sprockets simply slot onto it and are secured by a lockring.

Cassette hubs allow for wider spaced bearings and, with the latest sealed bearing hubs from manufacturers like UK-based Hope Technology, multiple sets of up to four bearings across the axle. There are hundreds of hub manufacturers who produce cassette and standard hubs for mountain bikes.

The main disadvantage with cassette hubs, especially now 8-speed has been adopted, is that because the hub flanges are closer together, to give enough room to fit on all the sprockets the wheel must be dished a lot more. This increases the difference in tension between the spokes on the sprocket side, which are very tight, and those opposite, which are slacker. As a result, if a spoke breaks that is under a lot of tension, the wheel will be thrown well out of true, while if there is insufficient tension in some other spokes, they are more likely to shake loose during a rough ride.

Always use small flange hubs: these require longer spokes and thus give more shock absorption. As a standard, 32 spokes give good, strong but light wheels, with a considerable weight saving over 36 spokes. If you are quite a light rider, consider using a 28-spoke front wheel.

Spokes

Double-butted stainless steel spokes are best as they 'give' a little and provide reliable strength that doesn't rust. They are thicker at the ends (butts) where the extra strength is needed. Plain gauge spokes are slightly heavier and provide a very rigid wheel – which is not always an advantage. The most popular double-butted gauge is 14/16 (2mm at the butts 1.8mm in the middle) although thinner ones are now available for the weight conscious.

Tender loving care

The quality of the three components of a wheel can be the absolute ultimate, but if they are not constructed with care and patience by a wheelbuilder who knows his craft, then the quality makes little difference.

OnZa porcupine tyres: very soft and grippy, hence very popular with downhillers

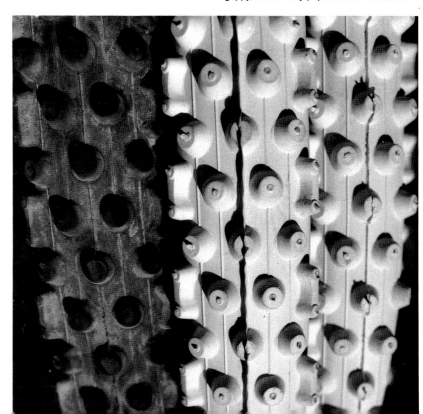

Tyres

Tyre widths used to be restricted to 1.5 inch section and fatter. Now if you wish, you can fit any size, making some excellent thin section mud tyres legal.

The most popular tyre choice is around 2inch: these cope with the majority of terrains pretty well. 1.5inch tyres are best in thick mud to increase clearance/grip. At the other extreme 2.1inch and above are needed when descents are very rocky and bumpy: with a large cushion of air the puncture risk is reduced and the ride more comfortable.

The traditional steel bead which seats the tyre onto the rim is now being replaced by Kevlar, which does the same job but is a lot lighter. Unfortunately the price is also higher, so you will have to decide if the weight saving is worthwhile.

The tyre casing is usually made from cotton thread, and depending on the number of threads per inch (TPI) the tyre is either lighter and more flexible (which means better cornering) or the opposite and a lot cheaper!

The rubber tread governs the surface you can ride best on. If the rubber itself is softer it gives better grip but wears faster, and vice versa.

The tread patterns can usually be slotted into one of three categories: road, multi-purpose and knobblies.

Road treads, as the name implies, are usually slick or semi-slick for on-road riding. Multi purpose treads usually have a solid centre ridge or one made up of small knobbles for all types of riding on- or off-road. Knobblies are purely for off-road use; depending on the tread design they are good in mud, loose sand, rock etc.

Tread design changes regularly, and once again fashion dictates which tyre is 'in' at any particular time, so the best advice is to try find out which is supposed to be best on the type of terrain you ride most on, or try to ride other bikes with different tyres to decide for yourself.

Whichever tyre you eventually go for, try to make sure that it fits well on the rim you are using and that if possible you can put it on and take it off by hand without tyre tools. This will help save you time during a race if you are unfortunate enough to get a puncture.

Inner tubes

We cannot leave the subject of tyres without a brief comment about inner tubes – after all, they hold the air and keep you mobile.

For racing, Presta valves are pretty much accepted as the standard, although Schraeder are still used and have the advantage of being able to be pumped up with a car footpump. Most quality cycle pumps are made for Presta, however, and they are easier to pump to a higher pressure, so our advice is to go for Presta.

Latex and butyl are the two materials used for tube construction. Butyl is the most common: latex is lighter, but gradually over a number of days air seeps out, and latex tubes are more expensive.

Imperforable tubes are also available. These are usually heavier, and are reinforced to stop thorns, glass, etc going through. Unfortunately most are still susceptible to pinch punctures, or snake bites, the commonest punctures during races. Snake bite protection inserts for wheels and reinforced side walls are being developed to help prevent this.

The first official downhill World Champion – Durango's Greg Herbold

Transmission

The transmission covers the drive chain – that is the chainset, front and rear derailleur, sprockets, chain and gear levers.

Compatibility between these components is a real minefield: often some things match, some don't! Ask yourself: will this chain run on these sockets with such a rear gear? How about these gear shifters and this front mech? And so on. To be totally safe, use the same make for all these bits especially if, technically, you are not too sure about how the various components work and match.

Back to basics: virtually all racing mountain bikes use three chainrings on the chainset to give the wide range of gears required to conquer the variety of courses you encounter on your travels. As a standard, 26-36-46 is a good start, and the only one you will need to change for extreme courses is the 26, perhaps to a 24 or 22 depending on how high the mountain is and how strong your legs!

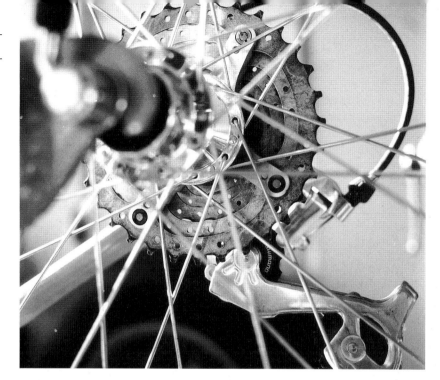

Always one step ahead of the competition, Shimano have an 8-speed cassette featuring drilled sprockets and an adaptor system to save weight over traditional sprockets. They have also introduced front chainrings with hooked teeth on the back of the chainring to aid shifting

John Tomac – the ad man's dream. 1991 World Cup winner and cross-country World champion

Chainrings should be round. A couple of year ago, Shimano produced elliptical chainrings designed to overcome top dead centre and to give more of the revolution on the downward stroke of the pedal, but they don't promote a good pedalling action and feel strange, especially if you use both road and mountain bikes, one with round rings and one with elliptical; so go for round.

Standard mountain bike cranks are 175mm in length – slightly longer than the standard 170mm on road bikes. This gives more leverage at slower speeds and low revolutions, but if you have very short legs you should use 170mm cranks.

There are usually eight sprockets on the back wheel, giving 24 gears in total. The normal range for the sprockets is 12-28, but again you can make changes, usually at the lower end, replacing the 28 with a 30 or 32 when required. Too wide a range at either front or the back will mean stretching the rear derailleur too much in order to take up the tension of the extra chain. The standard length Shimano rear derailleur will cope with 26-36-46 chainwheels and 12-28 sprockets easily. Over stretching the gears will damage the springs and mechanisms making shifting less smooth.

Linking the front and back sprockets and chainrings is the most abused part of any bike – the chain. Compatibility of the chain with the sprockets on the wheel is vital, so it's best to go for whatever the manufacturers recommend. Failing that, use a Sedis road chain: this will work on anything, even recently developed 8-speed cassettes, will last longer, and will probably be at least as reliable as the matching chain for the system.

Chains get incredible punishment and abuse on mountain bikes – the slower speeds and low gears put a lot of torque on the chain, not to mention crunching gear changes and attacks by mud, dust and dirt, and a chain failure in a race can be the end of your chances (and also painful!) So change your chain regularly, especially if you just use one bike for all your racing and training: once a month is reasonable and as they are not expensive it won't cost you the earth.

Ensure your chain length is correct so that you can use as many of the available gears as possible. Never use the extremes of the gears (big chainring/big sprocket or small chainring/small sprocket), as it puts increased tension on the chain as the chainline is too severe. However, you should be able to use the rest without any problems. Make sure that you can use the big chainring and the second and third OK, as on bumpy descents this

An underbar shifter from Shimano

The grip shift is a smaller version of the bullet and an alternative to the thumbshift gear change

keeps your chain under the most tension and stops it bouncing off.

Gear changing is by way of a thumb or trigger shift gear lever mounted on the handlebars for easy changing. It is 'indexed' with the rear mechanism to provide quick, precise changes. Most gear levers are matched to a rear gear to ensure that the mechanism moves the correct distance for each click of the lever, so make sure they actually do match.

The gripshift is a twist grip mounted on the handlebars, similar to the one that used to change the Sturmey Archer gears on your shopper! Gear changing with this is incredibly fast, and as you don't have to move your hand at all, it is possible to change instinctively, even when out of the saddle while climbing, which is a great advantage.

When indexed gears are working well they are a joy to use: crisp, silent changes even under pressure. On the other hand, if they are out of sync, worn or simply not clean or maintained, they can be a nightmare. Make sure you use the flexible prestretched gear cables and stiff non-compressible outer cables that are recommended, and keep the cable adjusted correctly by means of adjusters either on the mech or on the lever.

Pedals

The best pedal for mountain bike racing is the clipless step-in type pedal or 'spuds' named after the original SPD design.

SPD pedals were developed originally for road racers, and it was only a matter of time before somebody developed an off-road step-in pedal to save people the trouble of converting their road pedals for mountain bike use. Shimano entered the market first with such a product, which has many good features. The main advantage of their pedal is that you can clip into it on either side, avoiding the need to flick it over to get in.

Simply put your foot on it and snap the shoeplate in. The shoeplate is a very simple, small design which on the Shimano shoe is recessed into the sole to allow easy walking with the bike, without the problem of the plate slipping on rocks, etc.

Pedals with toe clips and straps are now reserved for the most traditional of riders; that said, they are still standard issue on most factory produced bikes. However, they still have their uses; trail rides, touring or in really muddy conditions where you spend more time running than riding. Clips and straps offer wide support for your feet and are better if you ride in trainers.

For serious use SPD type pedals will, combined with a stiff soled off-road shoe, offer the best power transfer from your feet to the rear wheel.

Shimano SPD clipless pedals are double sided to ease entry

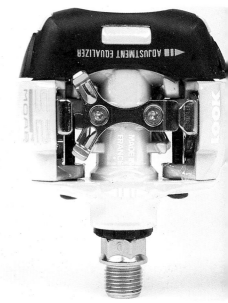

A MOAB pedal

As with all mountain bike components there are several manufacturers producing clipless pedals, e.g. Look, OnZa, Time, Tioga and Ritchey. Like every component area it's a growing market and re-designs are an annual occurrence.

Left: a Shimano SPD cleat recessed into the sole to allow easy walking; right: a conventional cleat with removable spikes ideal for steep, muddy run-ups

Space your clips out slightly so that the part the strap passes through does not jam behind the pedal back-plate if it is trodden on.

Brakes

The use of cantilever brakes that fasten to pivots brazed onto the frame is almost universal.

Manufacturers are developing hydraulic brakes, hub brakes and disc brakes, but they are still second best. Hydraulic brakes are getting better and more efficient, although still a bit on the heavy side. They are most used for trials riding and downhill racing, where mega-powerful brakes are a necessity. Disc and drum brakes are getting lighter by the year, and who knows what the future will bring? However, in the meantime, cantilevers offer the best combination of efficiency, lightweight and ease of adjustment.

Most cantilever brakes have a multiple adjustment for the brake blocks so that they can be raised, lowered or toed in and out. Make sure the straddle cable can be removed easily to open the brakes up so that you can remove the wheels without difficulty – you will need to be able to do this quickly if you get a puncture during a race.

If your boss on the frame has three holes to allow you to vary the tension on the spring of the brake, fit it on the slackest setting. This

A handlebar set up like this offers numerous positions. Just remember where your brake levers are

will ease the pressure on your braking fingers, especially on long descents.

The brake levers should be wide enough to get three fingers on for maximum braking power. Most have split adjusters so that the cables can be easily removed for re-lubrication. Tim removes the springs from his levers, again to ease the pressure on his fingers during constant braking on long descents.

New on the scene are 'servo-wave' brake levers. These have a cam inside that assists with braking 'modulation' which is the ability to increase braking forces gradually. Doubtless this advance in design will be developed further and

become more popular with other manufacturers.

Handlebars and stems

Most handlebars on production mountain bikes tend to be too wide. The right width has been shown to be around 21–22inches (54–56cm) so if your bars are wider than that, chop an equal amount off each end to come down to this optimum measurement.

Bars are made of various materials, but aluminium is the favourite. Both carbon fibre and titanium are also used for bars, but carbon fibre has not proved to be a successful material for such a critical component under high stress, and titanium is just plain expensive. Use a sensible weight bar as light bars can bend, especially if you're a heavy rider or ride downhill with suspension: a high-speed failure is not recommended.

Bar ends allow greater flexibility in your position on the bike, they let you spread out a bit on the flat and give you more leverage for climbing. There are loads of different shapes and styles now available to suit all kinds of riders' hands. Even more radical are bars which extend forwards until they eventually join, giving numerous position possibilities. It was bars like these that Ned Overend used in the 1990 World Championships.

Stems come in a variety of lengths and rises, and should be chosen primarily with position in mind. For racing, a flatter stem gives a better position, and around 100° or 110° (10° or 20° rise) is normal.

Again aluminium or chromoly are the best and lightest materials, and most stems come with some sort of cable hanger or routing for the

Handlebar extensions come in a variety of shapes and sizes and offer scope for different positions, mainly for climbing. Here Ned Overend chooses the traditional position

front brake cable. If not you will need a cable hanger under the locknut on your headset.

Also available on a handlebar stem is suspension. The 'flexstem' offers good suspension and shock reducing characteristics at a fraction of the cost of suspension forks, and will be worthwhile if your hands and arms suffer badly and the budget is limited.

You will need a handlebar grip on your bars, and a large number are available. The original 'Grab-On' grips are good but avoid 'Grab-On' copies as the foam is nowhere near as dense and they don't last long. Rubber is the favourite material. Get some which have a good grip, even when wet, and which are not so bulky that you cannot get your hands round them, especially if you have small hands.

To aid installation and removal of grips try a squirt of hairspray, it acts as a lubricant when wet and because it's lacquer it dries like glue, just the job.

Accessories

In addition to the basic components on your bike there are a number of accessories available: some a necessity some a luxury. The necessities include the bottle and cage, the pump, and the saddle pack.

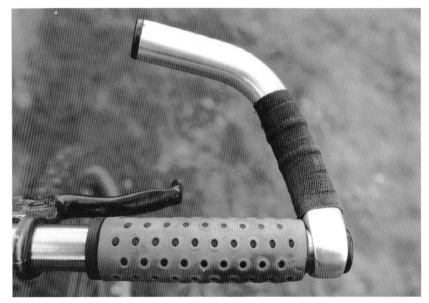

Curved bar ends like these by OnZa, are the best. They give a better hand position than straight bar ends, and they are less likely to get caught on course marker tape or stray branches

Front suspension at a fraction of the cost! If you cannot afford forks try suspension stems to reduce upper body fatigue caused by the constant vibration

The most useful of the 'luxury' add-ons is probably the handlebar-mounted computer. These usually have several functions, and can be handy, especially during training, to record your time, distance travelled, and speed – so you can know just how fast you really went down that 60-mph hill!

Bottle and cage
Of great importance during a race, especially in hot conditions, is a water bottle and a cage to fit it in. Two cages are normal, one on the down tube and one on the seat tube. If the course does not include a section where you need to carry the bike on your shoulder, you should leave both cages on; otherwise, remove the cage on the down tube to assist picking the bike up, and make sure the cage is a one-piece construction that will not deform out of shape or break as it is knocked against your body while being carried.

Make sure also that the bottle is a good tight fit in the cage to avoid losing it on bumpy descents.

Bottles come in two standard sizes: 500 ml and 800 ml. They have easy-to-open spouts which are pulled open with your teeth.

Pumps
Punctures, while not common, are nevertheless the curse of the mountain bike racer, and some means of inflating the new tube

16g CO_2 cartridge and adaptor

should be carried at all times to avoid a long walk.

For training, a standard pump – either frame-fitted or mounted on pump pegs – is adequate, but for racing consider using CO_2 canisters to speed up the process and get you back in the race as quickly as possible.

The CO_2 comes in a small cartridge. When connected via an adaptor screwed onto the valve, it inflates a replaced or repaired tube in a couple of seconds.

The cartridges come in 12, 16 and 25 gram sizes, depending on the size of the tyre to be inflated: 12 g is designed for 700 c road wheels, 16 g will inflate a 2.0-in tyre to about 35 psi (2.4 bar), and 25 g the same to about 50 psi (3.5 bar).

Saddle pack
The best place to carry your spare tubes and various tools is tucked away under your saddle. Numerous saddle packs are available; choose one large enough to take two inner tubes, a set of tyre levers, a CO_2 adaptor and two canisters, a chain riveter, a small multi-tool with screwdriver, an Allen key and a socket selection.

Weight-saving

Weight reduction is the holy grail for mountain bike racers, who constantly search for a way of saving a few grams here and there. Just as when buying hi-fi equipment to increase the quality slightly can sometimes double the

You can rely on John Tomac to set the trend in equipment: carbon frames, disc wheels, drop bars and suspension forks were all seen first being used and abused by Johnny T!

price, very slight savings in weight can cost a disproportionate amount, and usually reduce the bike's strength.

Unless money is no object (lucky you!), think carefully about where weight can best be reduced. If you have a basic heavy frame, putting titanium handlebars on won't make much difference to the overall weight, so decrease the weight of the frame and wheels first.

Always remember that a little more weight is not a bad thing if it brings

with it more reliability and strength. You cannot win races with broken or failed components, however light they are, so consider each purchase wisely.

Maintenance

A mountain bike is an expensive piece of equipment, and if treated well will last for quite a few years with only occasional replacement of worn components. However if it is in use constantly for training and racing it is easy to ignore the general upkeep. If carried out regularly, this only takes a short time each week, and will give you an opportunity to spot anything worn before if gives up the ghost on a ride.

If you race on a Sunday, make Monday, which is a light training day, the day to clean the bike thoroughly. If the race was knee deep in mud or water, give the bike a preliminary rinse after the race.

As you clean the bike on Monday, keep an eye out for anything loose, stiff, worn or broken: you have the rest of the week to sort it out before the next weekend's race.

If you have to train on the same bike all week, do a similar check on Friday, which gives Saturday to go to the bike shop.

Saturday night is not the best time to discover you need a new chain!

Mountain bikes take more abuse than any other bike, so learn to understand how your bike works and take pride in its appearance and upkeep; even if you aren't going to win, it is a lot more fun riding a well-maintained bike.

Cleaning a mountain bike

Try to develop a routine for cleaning your bike, and it will take only a matter of 20–30 minutes from start to finish.

Ideally you should use a workshop stand which supports your bike off the ground without the wheels in. If you haven't got one, improvise and hang the saddle from a line or even a tree branch.

For regular cleaning you will need:

- two buckets of water: one hot and soapy, one cold
- a stiff brush
- a sponge
- a pot of degreaser and a brush
- either a 'sleeping hub' or simply a screwdriver through the rear ends, to tension the chain with the wheels out.

The best degreasers are water-soluble and easily available at car-accessory shops, but petrol or a petrol/diesel mixture can also be used.

With the bike supported, drop the wheels out and use the degreaser on the freewheel sprockets and then on the chain, chainrings and derailleurs. Next, with the brush and hot water, scrub the awkward parts such as the brakes, pedals and under the saddle, and then use the sponge on the frame tubes, bars, stem and bottle cages. Start at the top of the bike and work down, so that by the time you get to the transmission a lot of the grime will have been removed by the water. Fill your sponge with water; turning the pedals, run the chain through the sponge to clean it thoroughly, and then wash the chainrings and gear mechs. Wash the wheels with the brush, and finally rinse everything off with cold water. Now the bike is ready to be dried and given a check-over.

Check the chain for wear by trying to pull it off the chainring teeth. It should move very slightly, but if you can pull it over half-way off the teeth, replace it.

Check the chainring teeth for 'hooking'. When worn, they go hook-shaped, and this causes slipping and chainsuck: the chain does not come off the ring, but follows it round and jams between the chainring and chainstay.

Look out for play in the headset, bottom bracket and wheels. If you find any, tighten them; best of all, if you have time, strip them down and re-grease them. To check for looseness in the wheels, lift the bike off the ground and move the top of the wheel from side to side: there should be no movement. For the brackets, hold the end of the cranks and try to rock them from side to side. For the headset, put the front brake on and rock the bike to and fro; again there should be no rattles.

Check the tyres for cuts and the wheels for buckles, and then move on to the brakes and gears. All cables should be free of kinks and frays and should run smoothly in the outer casing. If not, replace them. Brake blocks develop ridges if they don't hit the rim square, and these then stick and don't allow the brake to release smoothly. Check the blocks for excessive wear, and if necessary replace them or file the ridges off. If you get a lot of brake squeal and you are sure you don't have oil or grease on your rims, toe the brake blocks in at the front so that the front hits the rim first. There should be an adjustment on the brake to allow this, but if not it can be done by gently tweaking the block with a pair of mole grips, being careful! Finally, just go round with an Allen key and make certain that the seat pins, handlebars, brake and gear levers and toeclips are all tight. Use common sense with this and don't overtighten them, especially on light components with alloy threads.

Once a season it is worth having a full service and stripping the whole bike down to ensure that it is running smoothly for major events later in the season. A word of advice: don't fit anything new or different close to any major events. Even new cables settle in and stretch, so use equipment that you are familiar with and which is used but in top condition.

Positional adjustment

It may take you a while to find the most comfortable and efficient riding position. Deciding the reach of the bike (the distance from saddle to handlebars) is especially difficult. Saddle height is very important too, and research done on road-bike position can be of help here.

Very basically, for the novice rider, you should be able to pedal backwards when seated barefoot on the bike, with your heels on the pedals. If you can do this only by rocking from side to side on the saddle, you are sitting too high and should lower your saddle.

It is possible to work out a more precise height from your inside-leg measurement (crutch to floor in bare feet), by multiplying this figure by 0.885. This gives the recommended measurement from the centre of the bottom bracket axle to the top of the saddle. However, even this figure may not be the absolutely definitive answer, as different pedal and shoe thicknesses and individual pedalling styles can affect the optimum height. Use this calculation as a guide only.

Similarly, multiplying your inside-leg length by 0.58 can give an indication of the best frame size (measured from the centre of the bottom bracket to the top of the seat tube on a diamond-design frame).

As we have mentioned, a precise recommended value for the distance from the saddle tip to the handlebars is more difficult to give,

but if you ride a road bike you are generally looking for a distance equal to that from the saddle tip to the point half-way between the tops of the bars and the brake-lever hoods on the road bike. This is in the region of 1.5-2 in (4-5 cm) longer than the saddle-to-bar measurement on a road bike.

If you fit handlebar extensions to your bars, ensure that these do not stretch you out too far, and remember that you need a lot of weight over the back wheel on loose climbs to give traction, so

your saddle should be slightly further back than on a road bike.

The height of your handlebars will to some extent depend on the frame design, the height of the front end of the bike, especially if it has a sloping top tube, and the rise of the handlebar stem. The style for racing at the moment is quite a long, low position, and so most stems are dropped as far as possible into the frame: stems are getting flatter, around 100° (10° rise).

5 Clothing

Your clothing requirements at first will be pretty basic, but as your involvement grows and more time is spent cycling you soon discover the advantages of racing and training in purpose-made kit.

Advances in fabric development have totally changed cycling kit in just a few years. Wool and acrylic jerseys, real chamois inserts in shorts, baggy training bottoms: all have been laid to rest with the introduction of lycra, polyester mixes and fabrics such as Tactel which wick moisture away from the skin and keep you warm and dry.

For racing the requirements are pretty straightforward. As summer is the main season, you just need a pair of shorts, a short-sleeved jersey, track mitts, shoes and a helmet. Training is a different matter, as is racing in winter or early spring, when conditions can be grim and the choice of clothing can make the difference between an enjoyable race or productive training session and a miserable ride.

The only rule about race clothing is that you must wear a helmet. For the rest, you can make as minimal a fashion statement as you like!

Footwear

Until quite recently, before the days of mountain bikes, off-road racers riding cyclo-cross were forced to make do with either road shoes converted with a couple of studs in the heels and pieces of rubber fastened to the sole to give grip when running, or training shoes which by their very nature are far too soft and flexible for riding bikes in.

The occasional manufacturer dipped a toe in the market and withdrew it quickly when sales did not materialise, and it was only with the advent of mountain bikes, and more precisely with the boom in racing, that a good choice of suitable shoes became available off the shelf.

If you are racing seriously, avoid the mountain bike boots that are fine for trekking in the Himalayas but are total overkill for riding a bike.

Go for a shoe and look for the following features:

- a stiff sole from heel to ball of the foot, with a softer toe section to help you when running

- a good tread to give enough grip

- the facility to fit shoeplates for clipless pedals

- an upper that will not be affected by scuffs on rocks, etc

- most important – try to get a shoe that is comfortable.

Socks should always be worn, and cotton or wool mix are the most popular. Cushion-soled sports socks will probably prove to be too hot in summer, but might be a good idea if the weather is bad.

Whichever style you prefer, make sure you are wearing them when you choose your shoe so that you get a good fit.

Shorts

Shorts should either be part of a skinsuit or be the bib variety, which does away with the need for braces. Lycra is now the norm; it comes in a variety of different qualities, which affect the fit – so choose carefully.

Try to get synthetic chamois inserts which look and feel like the real thing, but which can be machine washed and dried quickly without ending up crispy – which is a sure way to start chafing problems on a ride.

Jerseys

Lycra skinsuits, consisting of shorts and jersey all in one, are popular. They are fine for short races or hillclimbs, but you are best using separates for longer races as you can make use of the pockets on the jersey for

food, and even spare tube and tools if you prefer to carry them on your person.

Always wear an undervest when racing; modern polypropylene vests take perspiration away from the body and keep you dry and comfortable. An undervest will also give you better protection in the event of a crash, as the two surfaces slide against each other and reduce grazing.

If the weather turns cold or if you race in the winter, wear lycra tights on your legs, a long-sleeved jersey or arm warmers, and some kind of chest protection – either a purpose made chamois leather or simply a piece of plastic under your jersey.

Gloves

Always wear track mitts when racing; they provide essential protection in the event of a crash and give good grip on the bars. The sort with gel pads in the palms are good for shock absorption too.

Helmet

Helmets are obligatory in races worldwide, and a must for all training off-road.

So when you get a helmet, get a good one!

For racing the helmet must conform to ANSI, SNELL or TUB standards. As 99 per cent of those available do conform to these standards, the choice comes down to comfort, weight and ventilation.

Choose the correct size, and ensure a good fit by using the additional foam pads that most helmets come with. Once this is done, adjust the retention straps to keep the helmet firmly in place.

If you race regularly in a hot environment, consider the ventilation properties of each helmet; don't just choose the nicest colour! Ventilation along the length of the helmet is best, with additional holes at the sides to give a good air flow over your head.

Glasses

Glasses are not so much to keep the sun out of your eyes as to provide good protection against dust and grit getting in your eyes – especially important early in the race when you are likely to be riding in a group. If the weather is really bright, and you aren't going into dark areas such as woods, standard dark lenses are OK, but more practical are clear lenses, or yellow if the day is dull.

Always keep your glasses on a string so you can let them hang for any periods you don't want to wear them: this is easier than trying to stuff them into a pocket and then finding they have bounced out just when you need them.

Warm-up gear

Warming up is a critical pre-race activity: the object is to get your body and muscles warm so that you are ready for the early efforts. For this reason it is better to wear too much clothing than not enough. The image of a race is always a nice bright warm day, but remember that race in March when you sat on the start line for 20 minutes watching your legs turn blue as the wind and rain howled across the start area! In Europe especially, even mid-July is no time to go to a race without a few extra layers of clothes in your bag, just in case.

If the weather is wet, don't warm up in any kit you intend racing in. Use spare shoes, warm bottoms, and waterproofs over your training top and hat. Change into dry clothes only when your course reconnoitring is complete. Even then, when you are riding around before the start, wear extra tops, and bottoms if you are able to remove them without taking your shoes off.

Some races are notorious for late starts, keeping you hanging around on the start line, so keep a top on until you are sure the start is imminent.

One useful addition to your bag is a pair of leg-warmers fastened with either a full-length zip or velcro; these can be left on until the last minutes before the start and then removed quickly. You will not be able to buy these as such, so find someone with a sewing machine to alter a pair for you.

Training kit

Your training kit will be similar to that which you warm up in.

In cold or wet conditions, pay attention to the extremities – head, hands and feet. Overshoes, gloves and hat will reduce heat loss, and even a pair of eyeshades (with clear or yellow lenses) can stop your face feeling as cold.

If you train in the dark, make sure you are highly visible to motorists by wearing light clothing and some kind of reflective belt or vest, and ensure you have good lighting and reflectors on your bike. And don't forget your helmet!

Philippe 'Darth' Perakis. Downhill racers need special protection, and if you don't win you can always take up American football

Rishi Grewal and Mike Kluge lead the charge: World Cup, Mammoth 1991

6 Race routine

You can probably remember your first race: you arrived either three hours too early to make sure you didn't miss it, or just as the race was lining up! You forgot your shoes, so rode in your friend's boots; stuffed yourself with chocolate for energy; didn't think to reconnoitre the course beforehand, and so rode over the drop-off half-way round that everyone else walked down because they knew it was there; punctured, and then found your pump was still on your training bike! You finished after someone lent you a CO_2 canister, with bloody feet, sore arms and dead legs, light-headed through hunger, and with a huge grin on your face! The fun was in doing the unknown, and once the pain had dispersed and you found out your finishing position of 237th, you drove home determined that the following week you would remember your shoes and make the top hundred.

There is a competitive spirit in everybody who races: if there wasn't, racing wouldn't be necessary and a steady Sunday ride would be enough. Even if you only train once a fortnight, you still set your own goals to make a certain position, or beat the guy who beat you in the last race.

It doesn't take long to get into a race routine, and once you find one, the fun of the unknown is replaced by the fun of competing to the best of your ability. No matter if you are a pro or a novice-class rider, it is still greatly enjoyable, and you can be satisfied if you gave it your best shot.

For the rider aspiring to greatness, the routine is important if the hours of training and attention to diet, sleep and exercise are to pay off. If you can arrive at a race knowing you have done everything right in the run-up to it, you can be confident of racing well without any worries.

What to take to a race

Tools and equipment spares can be kept together, but don't forget to replace a spare, if you use it, before the next race.

Try to be systematic about what you take to a race; in that way you are less likely to forget something. Here is a checklist:

- Spare wheels
- Spare tyres, including different widths and treads
- Spare inner tubes
- Different sizes of sprockets and chainrings
- Spare chain
- Selection of inner and outer cables
- Tools
- Saddle pack, including CO_2 canisters, tyre levers, chain riveter, multi-Allen-key/socket tool, inner tubes
- First-aid kit
- Safety pins for numbers
- Spare feeding bottles and drink mix
- Race food (Powerbars, energy bars, muesli bars etc.)
- Food for afterwards (sandwiches, cake, biscuits, canned drinks etc.)
- Embrocation box (including warm and hot cream and balm, chest rub, Olbas oil, sports wash and flannels)
- Bucket and sponge, brush, dry cloths, lube oil in spray and liquid form, insulation tape, tag ties for fastening numbers to bike

In addition, your race bag should contain the following:

- Helmet
- Glasses and a selection of lenses (yellow, clear or grey)
- 2 short-sleeved undervests
- Long-sleeved undervest
- Short-sleeved jersey
- 2 long-sleeved jerseys
- 2 pairs of shorts
- 2 training bottoms
- Leg warmers
- 2 tracksuit tops
- 2 pairs of shoes
- 3 pairs of socks
- 2 towels
- Track mitts
- Gloves
- Racing cape or waterproof jackets
- Headband
- Toilet bag, including embrocation remover
- Racing licence
- Chamois cream
- Flip-flops
- Plastic bags for wet or muddy kit

Preparation

Most races are still Sunday only, although a lot now take over the whole weekend, with either a qualifying race to determine the field and start order, or downhill, trials and slalom racing as a taster to the main cross-country on Sunday.

Your preparation starts on Friday, when you train lightly, if at all, and the bike is given a final check and polish. Friday is also an important night for a good sleep, as Saturday's may be interrupted by nerves as race-day approaches.

If possible, travel on Saturday so that you can have a leisurely and detailed look at the course for Sunday, especially if the circuit is a long one. The last thing you need on Sunday morning is a two-hour ride around the course! If you have to ride a qualification race on the Saturday, then this in itself is a good opportunity to look round, and unless it is a World Championship qualification you don't need to go round beforehand.

Checking the course

So what are you looking for as you check the course in advance? Look for hazards that are to be avoided, including large rocky sections that may cause punctures; quick routes that perhaps go off the main track; and your best lines around bends and on descents. Even look for a longer route if it means avoiding a problem: a longer way can sometimes be just as quick if it avoids dismounting and running.

Look for suitable sections of the course for taking a drink and eating. These usually need to be relatively easy so that you don't lose any time. If a helper is going to hand you up a bottle, agree on a place where you can see him or her easily.

Decide which chainring you intend to be on for each section of the course, especially where you need to be on the small chainring for hard climbs. This will help you to remember to change in good time and to avoid bad gear changes that could reduce you to walking.

Decide if your range of gearing is adequate – perhaps you could ride the big climb with a 26 chainring instead of the 28 – and whether the tyres you have on are the best for the conditions. If it rains, will it turn into a quagmire or will it drain and remain dry? Is the descent bad enough to warrant fatter tyres? Do you need to shoulder your bike? If not, will you want one bottle cage or two?

If you cannot pre-ride the course the day before, and the lap is too long to do on the Sunday morning, check out the bikes of people who have been round and see what they have decided to use. Also, find out if there are any hazards you should know about, especially any dodgy descents or obstacles that cannot be seen easily.

Make any changes to your bike you have decided on, and for the rest of the day try to rest and relax, and avoid too much walking about or too much sun. If it is going to be very hot, keep drinking to avoid dehydration.

Going . . .

. . . going . . .

. . . gone

On your pre-race ride of the course make sure you know what is under the water!

Obstacles built specifically for the event, such as temporary bridges, should be ridden cautiously. During the race their condition can alter drastically and bridges like this invariably become very slippery

Pre-race food

Nutrition for racing is covered in more detail in chapter 10, but here is some basic advice on what to eat before the race.

Saturday night is the time for a carbohydrate-packed meal to top up your energy levels. Some races provide pasta parties, an ideal way to do it. Pasta, potatoes, bread – all these are ideal as a base for the meal, but avoid any fatty or greasy items that will be hard to digest.

On Sunday morning, you should aim to eat your last meal three hours before you race. If the start time is midday or earlier, combine this meal with breakfast; if later, have breakfast and then your meal.

Breakfast should be normal and light: cereal or muesli, toast or bread, but with a bit extra if it is the pre-race meal such as an omelette or pasta if you can face it so early!

If you have trouble eating a reasonable quantity early in the morning, use some of the liquid meals that are available, but avoid anything fatty such as fried foods, or too much simple carbohydrate such as sugar or confectionery.

Final preparations

Give yourself an hour's rest to digest the meal, and then go for a ride: around the course if possible (don't forget there may be other races taking place), or part of it if the lap is too long. This will normally take around half an hour. When you get back, make any last-minute changes to your equipment if conditions have altered, and go and change into your racing kit with an extra layer to keep warm until the start.

At this time put any embrocation on your legs, especially if the weather is cold or wet, and with half an hour to go start your warm-up with some stretching and mobility exercises to ensure that all your muscles are warm and ready to go. If your start position has been decided by a qualifying race, you don't need to be at the start too early, but if it is a free-for-all, get to the line with about 15-20 minutes to go and try to get a good position on the line. If there are a couple of hundred people in your race the start is especially important if you are to get away well and not be held up on any narrow sections of the course behind slower riders.

Obstacles soon after the start, such as this river crossing, can cause big hold-ups. Try and start as fast as possible to avoid the inevitable queues

Race tactics

You should have checked out the start area on your pre-race rides and will know the fastest or smoothest line to take.

The start in a mountain bike race is not as vital as in a cyclo-cross, as the distance is a lot further and more opportunities are available to pass easily and to make up time. However, it is silly to give away a time advantage to your opponents for no reason, so try to concentrate on being near the front, while not necessarily hammering away into the lead.

If the race is going to be a long one, settle down into a rhythm quickly and ride at a pace you know you can keep up for the whole time. Don't start fast and blow up after only a short distance, as you will continue to struggle for the rest of the race. If you find the pace hard but you are in a leading group of riders, let them lead while you follow and see if they look as though this will be the pace for the whole distance or if it is just an opening burst. If you feel confident of taking up the pace, then do so: out in front is the best place to be, as you have a clear line and can ride at your own pace. Don't be pushed into going too hard too soon, though – you need to know yourself and at what pace you can race.

If you are further down the field, try to pick off the people in front of you steadily. If you can see someone in front, try to catch him or her up by the top of the hill, for example, or by the end of the road. When you catch up, follow for a short while until you recover from the effort, and then pass and do the same to the next person. If you are struggling to stay with someone, whether at the front or the back of the race, stay behind and let the other rider set the pace, and hope you can find an opportunity to get past towards the end of the race.

If you know the attributes of the people you are with, try to exploit their weaknesses and do not play to their strengths. For instance, it is no good sitting behind someone you know to be a better sprinter than you – you must try to leave such an opponent before the finish. Similarly, if you are a better descender, you should take the lead on descents to avoid being baulked, and hopefully you can leave your opponent behind. Don't attack anyone on a flat stretch. It is a lot easier for your opponent to respond to and stay with you on the flat, so try uphill, or over a tricky section – or just before a descent, which can surprise your opponent and give you a few seconds' advantage which you can extend on the descent.

Whichever method you use, don't forget to drink!

Don't forget to drink regularly. In the heat of the battle it is too easy to forget, and if it is hot dehydration can affect your performance considerably and can even be dangerous. It is hard to put a figure to the quantity you should drink, but as an example Tim drinks a bottle about every half hour in warm weather, so you can see that one bottle will not last you a two-hour race!

If you have trouble during a race, such as a puncture, it is important to stay calm, repair it as quickly as possible, get back into the race and try to return to your former position. If you puncture early in the race, don't make the mistake of going flat out trying to pass people too quickly. Instead, keep under control and concentrate on picking people off: remember, the two minutes you lost changing the tube

will be very insignificant towards the end of a long race when the gaps between riders can be a lot more. All that happens if you go too fast is to increase the chance of puncturing again, or even crashing, simply through trying too hard. Keep cool! If it happens towards the end of a race it is a different matter, and you can afford to expend a bit more energy in your fight to regain your lost ground, as you will have less to lose.

Afterwards

When you have finished the race, don't hang around in your racing kit, which will probably be wet and make you lose heat rapidly, especially if the weather is cool. If you are required for a presentation, you will have a while to get some extra clothes on, have a quick wash and a drink before you are needed. If you aren't required, put a top on and have a drink and a rest. The hour following a race is the best time to replenish your muscles' glycogen (energy) store, so if possible have something to eat, or if you don't feel like it, have a high carbohydrate drink instead. If you are cold or wet, don't wait around – go straight off and get changed and warm.

Some riders handle altitude better than others. Henrik Djernis is one of the rare Europeans who can compete at over 9,000 feet and still pose a threat

Racing at altitude

If you live in the lowlands of Europe or America, racing at higher altitudes can be a problem, as many riders found in the 1990 World Championships in Purgatory, Colorado, held around 9000 ft (2700 m). It is not possible simply to turn up and race, as many of the Europeans found when they arrived during the week before the race: you need to acclimatise to the thin air.

You begin to notice the effect of height at around 4000-5000 ft (1200-1500 m), and from 7000-8000 ft (2100-2400 m) and above, a period of acclimatisation of at least 2-3 weeks should be planned.

For the first few days you will feel very breathless and will find sleeping and eating a problem; feelings of lethargy and irritability are common. It is vital to build up your riding slowly under these conditions, to take note of how you feel, and to look after yourself.

More fluid is lost at altitude, and so you must rehydrate regularly, especially during and after training. The effects of the sun are more pronounced, too, so use sun-block cream, and wear something on your head to shade your neck.

It has been found that carbohydrates are used up at a higher rate than at sea level, so ensure your diet is rich in carbs, or take carbohydrate supplements. Also, take an iron supplement, as the production of red cells in your blood is increased.

The effects of altitude combined with jet-lag can make you feel like death warmed up and leave you wondering how you can possibly race, but given time and a steady build-up, the effects will gradually lessen. Unfortunately, in three weeks you will never acclimatise to the extent of someone living at that height, but at least you will be competitive, and sooner or later you can have a return match at sea level and put them in their place!

7 Techniques

Basic racing techniques

Established racers – move on! By now you have got beyond the awkward stage in breaking, cornering, climbing and descending in race situations. All you need is to refine and perfect what you can already do, shaving off the odd second here and there. For professionals like Tim, the basic techniques have become second nature, and they have a hard time explaining what they do when, say, approaching a bend or climbing a hill. Novice riders, however, need a proper understanding of basic riding techniques, which you will refine yourself when you've got a few more hours in race situations under your belt.

The two most important ingredients for a mountain bike racer are fitness and skill. As a beginner, you may not possess vast quantities of either, but you need to improve them in line with each other, and regular off-road

With technical skills refined from his BMX days Tinker Juarez is a fine example for any up-and-coming rider to copy

riding will do just that. Road racers are very fit – as fit as the best mountain bike racers – but because their off-road techniques are not so good they rarely win mountain bike races straight off; they have to master the different skills. Conversely, trials competitors are super skillful, but would be blown away on the first climb of a mountain bike course because their particular discipline doesn't require the same high levels of fitness.

The techniques required to ride certain parts of a course, or over certain terrains, will be learned as your experience grows. If you train and race on as many different types of terrain as possible, you will not be taken by surprise by the conditions you may encounter during a race. Circumstances may make this difficult: your area may be flat and sandy, for instance, and the only chance you have to ride on hills and over rocks may be during actual competitions. In this case, it is doubly important to pre-ride the course, preferably the previous day, to practice the terrain and solve some of the problems you will meet. If you are

lucky enough to be able to ride in an area with a good variety of terrain, make the most of it and don't limit your training rides to the same routes all the time. You may get to know these routes too well and will then run the risk of losing the ability to 'sight read' the ground in front of you, and will be unprepared for surprises. Variation in your training routes is also more stimulating mentally, preventing training sessions becoming a bore.

Watch the pros ride, if you are not in their race, and see how they tackle different obstacles. Look at the line they take down hills and round corners; see how smoothly they mount and dismount; then simply try to copy them. Videos of races are helpful in learning techniques, as you can rewind and replay them until you get the idea, and then go out and put it into practice.

Balance

Balance is the key to a lot of mountain bike techniques, especially at lower speeds; at higher speeds it is still important, but is then probably more correctly

thought of as correct weight distribution than balance.

Riding over rocks, logs, kerbs, bunny-hopping, even riding up steep hills, balance is the difference between success and failure (although of course for the steep uphills fitness is of equal importance!) Spend some time 'playing' on your bike at low speeds to find out what you can and cannot do. Simple tests like turning in as tight a circle as possible, trying to pull a wheelie, or riding along the edge of a kerb are all good ways to find out your limits. Try all your exercises both sitting on the saddle and standing on the pedals to discover which way they work best; also try them in different gears to see if that makes a difference.

When you are confident at low speeds (or, more likely, bored with them!) get off-road and try the same exercises a bit faster, on some slopes. Practise all the theories you have read about; find out for yourself what happens if you brake whilst cornering, or turn your handlebars to corner instead

Play on your bike. Learn what you and your bike can and cannot do: then if you are faced with an unusual obstacle in a race situation you will be able to handle it more confidently

of leaning your body, or descend sitting down, rather than slightly out of the saddle ... For climbing, try the same hill first sitting in the saddle and then standing on the pedals to see which gives the most traction; then try it in different gears, and see which gets you up there fastest. If you want to succeed in competition, you have to explore the potential of your bike to the full, in every possible type of terrain, so you know exactly what it will and will not do; eventually, what you are aiming at is becoming as one with your bike.

Braking

In time, the art of controlling your speed so you can negotiate a hazard – a corner, a switchback descent, a steep descent, or whatever – will become second nature. But for the novice racer, braking is a major issue, so it's worth spending some time thinking about how and why you brake and practising until you are absolutely familiar with the way braking affects the handling of your bike under all conceivable circumstances.

First things first: make sure you know which side your back and

Even champions have to brake! Here Ned Overend brakes hard with the back (right hand) brake and feathers the front, avoiding heavy front braking on such a deep, loose surface

front brakes are on. Sounds obvious, I know, but if you use more than one bike and they came off-the-peg they may have the brakes on different sides.

Secondly, think through your reasons for braking. It is simply to reduce your speed by just enough to negotiate a particular obstacle, not to decelerate so suddenly that you are thrown over the bars, or lock your wheels. The most underused part of many a novice rider's bike is the front brake, the reason being a quite understandable fear of flying over the handlebars, but in fact for this to happen you would need to be travelling down a steep slope quite slowly, then slam on the front brake, and throw your body-weight forward – not a normal procedure during a race!

The front brake offers the most powerful braking force, but unfortunately using your front brake reduces the manoeuvrability of your bike. If you need to steer a line round an obstacle on a steep descent, what you do is ease off the front brake while you negotiate the obstacle, braking only when the bike is travelling in a straight line. Most effective braking is achieved by 'feathering' the front brake lightly, usually in conjunction with the back brake. On steep descents, the best grip offered by a tyre is just before it locks up and slides, so what you should do is brake heavily with the back, up to just before locking point, and then add light front braking if the speed is still too high.

To practise negotiating obstacles whilst braking, set up a slalom course on a steepish slope using whatever natural obstacles you can find, and experience the effects of heavy braking on slow corners. You will eventually learn how to apply pressure to your brakes smoothly, keeping the back wheel rolling, not sliding too much, and applying and releasing the front brake, controlling your speed whilst still turning.

The art of good braking is anticipation; by anticipating the need to brake you can keep it smooth and under control, rather than having to grab at the brakes at the last minute. For steep drops, control your speed on the approach so the braking on the drop is to maintain that speed, never to reduce it. Of course for bends, all braking is done on the approach to the bend, and the bend taken brakes off to aid acceleration away from the bend.

Climbing

In theory, climbing hills on a mountain bike is easy – lots of low gears, plenty of grip – that's what they were built for, isn't it? So how come it's so hard? Well, usually it's down to strength and fitness, but correct technique plays a big part too, especially as the hills get steeper. How many times have you ridden up a hill – panting hard, but getting on OK – only to have

to put a foot down when you lose your balance on a tricky bit?

The problem generally is in trying to steer a course uphill. The normal climbing position is seated, weight back on the saddle to aid traction, with very little weight over the handlebars. It is this last factor that is the difficulty – when you try to steer you turn the wheel too far, then you try and correct it, and the result is a quick zig-zag and a sudden stop.

Instead of steering forcefully round obstacles, try to pick a line that avoids them and change your line by shifting your weight and using a light touch on the bars. Standing on the pedals is also a good way to make changes of direction. Remember your 'tight turning circle' exercise? It was easier to do standing on the pedals; similarly, standing on the pedals whilst climbing means more weight on the bars and gives you greater ability to swing the bike round. The disadvantage of standing on the pedals for a climb is that less weight is over the back wheel, which results in reduced traction and the risk of wheel-spin. Try and keep low out of the saddle, back quite flat, arms bent, and 'attack' any steeper or looser sections, increasing speed momentarily until you are back in the saddle again.

On longer climbs, the easiest mistake for the novice to fall into is to set off too fast and run out of steam halfway up. If you are unsure of the length of a climb, set off at a steady pace, in an easy gear, sitting in the saddle and maintaining a steady climbing rhythm. Eventually you will develop a sense of pace and know what speed or effort you can continue with, but until you do it is better to go too easily and have something left at the top, than to be reduced to walking before you get there.

Good position, constant rhythm and concentration are important factors in climbing long hills

Europeans Anne Caroline Chausson and Caroline Alexander lead the assault on the American stranglehold of women's racing

Descending

For the majority of mountain bike fans, fast descents are what it is all about, and any amount of suffering on the way up is more than made up for coming down!

Your skill and nerve are the main factors limiting the speed of your descent. Try to stay relaxed, not tense or stiff. This way, you will be better able to absorb the shock of bumps and rough ground and you won't get bounced about so much.

On fast descents, look ahead a few seconds so you are in a position to anticipate what is coming up and act accordingly – braking, accelerating, changing gear or simply changing your line of descent. Cornering on fast descents is a matter of checking your speed on the approach to the bend and taking the right line. Any braking should be done on the approach to the bend, not through it, and the right line is the one that cuts across the apex of the bend, making it as straight as possible to avoid too much steering, or leaning, or reducing your speed.

Steep, slow descents are a different matter altogether. They

Descending fast requires nerve and skill. Keep your weight well back, stay relaxed and concentrate on the ground a few metres in front of you

Britain's Fred Salmon experiences the pain involved in going uphill fast

require heavy braking to keep speed down and as much weight as possible over the back wheel to keep the tyre gripping and reduce sliding. Some obstacles on the way down a hill are better tackled by speeding up than by slowing down, as any bumps or holes are likely to cause a bike that is moving very slowly to grind to a complete halt, whilst you continue gracefully onwards ... Go a bit faster, and the momentum will carry you through. Check your speed before you start the descent; it is too late to brake once you are on your way down.

Changing gear

Gears always change more smoothly when they are operated without a full load on. This means anticipating your changes rather than waiting until you are straining on a climb before making a change. If you're not sure whether you will need to change gear, remember that it is better to be in too low a gear than too high; you can always change up if you are spinning too quickly.

Try to be always aware of what size gear you are using, and work out beforehand which chainring you will need for particular sections of the course so you don't have to make rushed, difficult changes.

Remember the practice of playing on your bike? Hopefully you will have learnt what you can ride and what requires a dismount, so you can avoid situations like this

Advanced racing techniques

Climbs are where the majority of races are won or lost, so assuming that you have the necessary basic techniques and the required level of fitness we will now consider the techniques for getting up hills in more detail.

Short, steep climbs

The speed you climb a short, sharp slope is all to do with the speed at which you approach it, so you should attempt to sprint hard towards it and let your momentum take you up. This requires power. You should use quite a big gear on the approach and on the climb to avoid wheel-spin. Riding out of the saddle is normal for this type of climb.

You can afford to go into oxygen debt on a climb like this, as it will be very short and you can recover over the other side, but you will face problems if you get to the next climb and find you haven't fully recovered – if this happens, change the training slightly and introduce some interval work to bring down your recovery rate.

Long climbs

These are the ones that do the damage and where the gaps grow, so be prepared to suffer the pain: remember that if it is hurting you it is hurting everyone else too, even the guys at the front.

You need to ride at a maintainable pace: at a pace just slightly below that which would take you into oxygen debt, and at which you can continue to the top. It is pointless to go too fast on the early part of the climb, only to blow up and lose more time on the second half.

Ride sitting in the saddle, but stand up occasionally to stretch your legs and back, and to increase your speed over slightly steeper or rockier sections. Sometimes it is necessary to go over the brink into oxygen debt, for instance to overcome a hard section remaining on your bike, or if you want to drop somebody. However, you should only do this if you are able to recover sufficiently quickly to get back into your rhythm, otherwise you would need to slow down so much to recover that you would lose more time than you had initially gained.

You need to choose a gear that makes you pedal at a faster rate than you would on the flat. Don't try to manage on too big a gear, as a slight increase in the gradient will mean either a gear change under pressure, which is not a good idea, or having to dismount, which is to be avoided if possible.

On very steep sections, the two major problems are keeping your front wheel down and your back wheel gripping. This is all about distribution of weight. To stop your front wheel from lifting, bend your arms, drop your head and shoulders slightly, and shift some body weight forward. To reduce wheelspin, pedal smoothly and without a jerky or erratic style, and move back on your saddle to keep the weight on your back wheel. If it is possible to approach a steeper section a bit faster, this is an advantage, as your momentum will carry you through better.

Climbing fast hurts like hell. You must accept this and come to terms with the heavy breathing and pain. The only way these will go is by slowing down, and if others can put up with it and you can't, they are going to beat you – it's as simple as that!

Very occasionally you will be forced to dismount because the track is too rough or too steep. If it is too steep but still a good smooth surface, push your bike until the track levels out sufficiently for you to remount. If it is all rough or very rocky or muddy, it is best to shoulder your bike, as this will be quicker than trying to push it over or through the problem area.

If you push, try to keep your body upright, and resist the temptation to crouch over the bars, as this constricts your breathing and just makes things worse.

Balance and weight distribution are important factors for both climbing and descending. Here you can see perfect balance to give optimum traction through the back wheel whilst keeping the front wheel down; a straight, uncramped body makes it easier to breathe while climbing, and is equally balanced for fast descents, slightly off the saddle with arms and legs bent to absorb shock

Descending

What goes up must come down, and descending rapidly and safely is a matter of skill and nerve. The skill can be learned, but the nerve is either there or not. If it's not, then you may never become a Tomac, but by improving your skills your confidence will increase. Then you can at least be sure you will not lose time descending, you just won't be able to make the race-winning move on the descent!

For short, steep hills, keep the pedals horizontal, stand on them and shift your weight right back. Use both brakes – the back mainly, the front gently – to avoid going over the bars. Hold on tight, especially if it is very bumpy, as a hand coming off the bars, or a foot coming out of a toeclip, can have disastrous consequences.

If you are in any doubt about a really steep descent, don't be afraid to hop off and run down, especially if you are in among a group of riders, as crashes will be that much more common with people descending at different speeds. Hold onto the bars and saddle, or the top tube, and run down using the bike as something to lean on.

For the more common long, fast descent, you will be pedalling, so

On steep, loose descents sit well back, slightly off the saddle. Lock the back wheel if necessary but avoid heavy braking with the front. Your concentration must be total

will be on the big chainring, and probably the small sprocket if the descent is very fast. On any sections that are bumpy and where you are not pedalling, change gear in anticipation onto a bigger sprocket (still on the big chainring) which will keep your chain tight and stop it coming off.

Concentrate on picking the right line and going as fast as possible. Look ahead for obstacles in your path, and try to ride smoothly. Fast descents can mean punctures from hitting rocks or holes, so keep an eye out and avoid these where possible. Be 'light' on your bike, and jump anything you cannot avoid, taking the pressure off the tyres, even if you don't clear the obstacle completely. Keep the bike mostly on the ground, though: save the fancy crossovers and big air for your fun rides – they might look good but they slow you down and increase the chance of crashing or puncturing.

For obstacles such as water bars, or ditches crossing the track, you should know from your course reconnoitring the shallowest part and the best line through, so they shouldn't come as a surprise. Brake as you *approach* them, not when you are on top of them, so that you can accelerate away quickly. If you jump, make sure you don't land front wheel first, or you will be picking dirt out of your teeth for the rest of the race!

The best descenders are confident. Approaching obstacles

too slowly is as bad as too fast: you get thrown around much more, whereas enough speed can carry you over much better. Don't think about crashing! If you think you are going to fall, the chances are that you will, as you freeze and go to pieces. Be confident!

Cornering

Corners on descents should be taken as straight as possible to avoid the need for slowing down. Any braking should be on the

On fast corners, stick to the smoothest line – it is usually the fastest

approach to the bend, not as you are cornering, so that you are in full control as you go round, and are accelerating as you leave the corner.

Don't steer round corners by turning the handlebars: it should all be done by leaning, because any turning of the front wheel will soon make it disappear from under you. If the corner is tight, put the outside pedal downwards and put

a lot of weight on it, keep the inside leg bent and point the knee out slightly.

If the corner is fast, you can keep the pedals horizontal and adopt a low tucked position like a downhill skier, and corner by leaning. Sitting up slightly can control your speed without the need for braking, and is also good for cooling you down!

On switchbacks, the shortest route is not the best, and you need to take a line which will minimise the gradient as you turn. The shortest time you are facing directly down the steep part of the corner the better, and as this means turning very tightly it can be a help to take one foot out of its toeclip to pivot the bike on, or to dab on the ground if the bike starts to slide away. If the corner is too tight or steep it can be quicker to jump off and run round the corner, or even to jump down and miss the corner altogether if the marking tapes do not direct you right round it. Again, you should work all this out before the race and decide which method is quickest.

If the corner is cambered, take advantage of it and use the camber to corner on. This means you don't have to decrease speed much, and gives you a fast exit from the corner.

Mounting and dismounting

The ability to jump on and off your bike easily is a very quick skill to learn, and very useful for a mountain bike racer. Eventually you will encounter something to make you get off, and the chances of this happening will increase if you are riding in a large field, as congestion occurs going into obstacles. It can be very handy to jump off, run past those who are trying to ride, and jump back on again.

You can save a lot of time on obstacles that are unrideable, such as ditches or low hurdles, or perhaps fallen trees, if you can dismount, clear the obstacle, and mount again in one fluid motion without losing speed.

If you come from a cyclo-cross background this will be second nature to you, as 'cross is based on disruptive obstacles, and the ability to master these techniques is important to all cyclo-cross riders.

Dismount at speed

Let us assume that you are riding along a fast track and have to clear a log that has fallen across and is too big to bunny-hop or ride over.

Hopefully you won't slow down too much, so don't bother changing gear. As you approach the log, swing your right leg over the saddle and put it between the frame and your left leg; your left foot is still in the pedal. Place your right hand on the top tube 2-3 inches (5-8 cm) in front of the seat pin, and lean your body back.

With a lot of weight going through your right arm, pull your left foot out of the toeclip and land right foot first on the ground, lifting the bike up with your right arm as you do so. Clear the obstacle, put the bike back on the ground as straight as possible, put your right hand back on the bars, and jump on.

If you use shoeplates, unclip the one on your left foot as you approach the log, so that the slot is not locating on the pedal plate, and just leave your toe in the toeclip. This will then slide out easily when you jump off. If the shoeplate is left on the pedal, it can stay where it is – and you will gracefully head-butt the log!

Dismounting like this takes practice. The best way to do it is to start off slowly, and gradually increase the speed and decrease the number of steps required before and after the log. The good guys can do the whole thing in just four steps, but this takes skill so don't be surprised if you need ten at first. The more time on your feet, the more speed you lose: aim for four and it will come with time!

One word of warning: don't take your left foot completely out of the toeclip and ride on the other side of the pedal, as it can easily catch on the ground, especially if this is bumpy; this will damage the pedal and fetch you off.

Dismount uphill

If you need to dismount uphill you will not be travelling fast enough to use the above method, so simply swing your right leg over the saddle as you push down on your left pedal and jump off. Don't forget to unclip your shoeplate, and don't try to put your right leg between your left leg and the bike, as you will lose too much momentum.

Dismount in good time, well before the obstacle you need to clear, and keep moving. Don't just ride until you stop and then climb off and start pushing: keep it all flowing, and you will lose far less time.

Remounting

If your bike is on your shoulder, you need first to get it onto the ground smoothly. Put your left hand on the bars, slide the bike off your shoulder onto your forearm and then onto the ground. Try not to drop it too heavily or you can derail the chain. Put your right hand on the bars, run a couple of steps and make sure you are under control, but still moving forwards, before you jump back on. Swing your right leg over the saddle, landing on the inside of the top of your thigh. Don't just jump and hope – you can do yourself some serious damage!

If you had dismounted correctly, your right pedal will be pointing forwards in just the right position to push down, flicking your feet into the toeclips or locking the clipless cleats in as you do so.

To dismount for an obstacle, swing your right leg over . . .

. . . place between left leg and bike (note left foot is halfway out of toeclip)

. . . land, pick up your bike by its downtube

. . . *place on shoulder* . . .

. . . and run up hill

To mount, reverse procedure, take the bike off your shoulder . . .

. . . put (don't drop it!) on the ground . . .

. . . place both hands on bars and jump on, landing on inside of top thigh

Carrying the bike

If the ground is rough when you have dismounted, or the gradient is too steep for you to push the bike, or perhaps you need to cross a river, then you will need to carry the bike on your shoulder.

Unlike cyclo-cross bikes, which are relatively easy to run with, mountain bikes have a few disadvantages which make things more difficult. First, they can be heavy! Secondly, frame design, especially on small frames, can reduce the size of the main triangle and make it hard to get the bike on your shoulder. Also bottle cages can get in the way, as can pumps.

Decide before the race how much carrying will be needed, and decide where to put your bottle cages. If it is hot and the lap is long you will need to keep both on, but perhaps you can put only one on your bike and the other in a pocket. The seat tube is the best place for a single bottle cage if you carry the bike a lot, as it leaves the down tube free for picking up.

The finest mountain bike racer of the eighties and still at the top – Ned Overend

You can pick up the bike either by the down tube or by the top tube. Swing it onto your shoulder; depending on your size, you will have to work out where you are going to put your right hand. If possible, put your arm under the down tube so that the bike rests on your forearm, and hold the left-hand grip or brake lever. If you can't reach the bars with this method, find one which enables you to hold the bars steady as you run, and which doesn't force the weight of the bike forwards – don't end up with the seat tube or top tube on your shoulder and the front wheel pointing down. The top tube should remain level, with the weight of the bike well back, making you run with an upright stance.

Bunny-hopping

The ability to bunny-hop – to clear an obstacle with both wheels off the ground – can be very useful; it saves having to slow down or dismount, and can save the situation if you are faced at speed with an obstacle you cannot slow down for, such as a fallen rider!

The guys who do trials competitions can clear crazy heights, up to 40 in (1 m), but during a race don't attempt

The most talented off-road rider in the world, cyclo-cross World Champion and twice silver medallist in the World Championship cross-country, Switzerland's Thomas Frischknecht

91

anything higher than 8-12 in (20-30 cm) or wider than 12-18 in (30-45 cm), such as a ditch.

Timing is critical, as is sufficient speed as you approach; keep your pedals horizontal, and if you get the chance tighten your toestraps slightly to reduce the likelihood of a foot flying out. Jump both wheels simultaneously, lifting bars and feet upwards together. If your approach is slower, lift the front wheel slightly before the rear, and try to avoid the back wheel hitting the obstacle.

Clipless pedals are a big advantage for bunny-hopping, as you can pull upwards with a lot more force than with a toeclip.

Ground conditions

Rocks

Rocks should be avoided wherever possible – they cause punctures! If the course is rocky, pump your tyres up hard (50 psi; 3.5 bar) and lose a bit of comfort and traction. Hit rocky sections at speed and try to coast over them – you probably won't be able to pedal as you will be bouncing about too much. If you have to pedal, use a big gear.

Keep your eyes open later on in a race, when you've done a few laps, as the routes other riders have taken around rocks will become

apparent. Rocks get knocked out of the way and routes get smoothed out.

If you come across a rocky section on a descent, it is sometimes better to hop off and run down it, rather than spend time trying to work out a route down or risk crashing or puncturing. If a course is particularly rocky, and you have access to suspension forks, use them: they can considerably reduce fatigue in hands, arms and shoulders.

If you know beforehand that a course is going to be muddy, fit narrower tyres to increase clearances, shorten your chain to keep it tighter on the small chainrings, and possibly even slacken your brakes off slightly, again to increase clearance.

Softer tyres give more grip, so bear this in mind if there are muddy slopes to ride up.

Mud slows everything down, so be prepared for a slog! You can't get completely out of the saddle as much, as you would simply lose traction, but a riding style slightly out of the saddle and further back can help. Let the bike take its own line through the thick bits, and don't fight it. Get used to the bike moving about – only experience will tell you what is OK and what is too much.

Concentrate on the line you are taking through mud – is it the quickest, or is there a longer route

Don't blindly follow the obvious route through deep mud. Keep an eye out for a longer, drier route. If a dry route isn't available, go for the puddles to keep clogging to a minimum

The majority of the top riders are now using clipless pedals, but even they keep an alternative in their bag if the course calls for some running, or the surface is one that might jam the release mechanism

that is drier (and therefore quicker)? In a well-attended race, soft ground can churn up very quickly, and deep ruts develop, so if this is likely to happen, try to work out an alternative way through for later laps.

Consider your choice of footwear and pedals very carefully if a course is muddy; some makes of clipless pedals do not operate well in mud, and the corresponding shoes can prove to be too stiff to run in for any distance – clips and straps may be a better option here.

If there are any wet sections of mud, or puddles, ride through them, as the water will loosen the mud off that is already on your bike and wheels.

Avoid very sticky bits – it may be as fast to ride, but you run the risk of clogging everything up, so jump off and run through.

In thick mud, if you are forced off, always run with your bike on your shoulder. Never push it: it is just too hard to do, and the mud carries on clogging up tyres and gears as you go. Put it on your shoulder, bearing in mind it could be very heavy; and, as you go, scrape the worst off with your hands. It doesn't sound too glamorous, but it has the right effect! You can even squirt

water out of your bottle onto the sprockets if they fill up: it all helps.

Deep, loose ground

On any sandy, loose surface, again let the bike go where it wants and don't fight it by steering. Try to travel in straight lines, as cornering is very awkward.

Fit fatter tyres, as they give a better ride – the tyre pressure doesn't really affect things much.

Don't use too sticky a chain lube, as sand can grind away chains, chainrings and sprockets in no time. Spray it on and wipe the plates dry, or even use a dry chain if conditions are very bad. Unfortunately sand means a major clean afterwards, or the bike feels gritty for ages.

Fast ground

On flat, firm ground, try to go as fast as possible without using too much energy. If possible sit behind somebody, use a big gear, and take the opportunity to drink plenty or to eat, if it is a long race. If you are on your own, get into an aero

In the countryside it's not only nature you need to look out for!

'time-trial' position, and don't lose concentration or you will find yourself slowing down.

8 Training

If you are just starting out racing mountain bikes, training routines can be very confusing: you realise you must train to improve, and you read somewhere that Tim Gould trains for five hours on a Wednesday, so after work you try to do five hours; but after only two you are shattered, and crawl home to bed wondering how you can possibly ever be good if you can't manage a five-hour session.

Rule number one: never copy anybody else's training routine, especially the good guys. They evolve training routines that are right for them over a number of years, and gradually accustom their bodies to the stresses involved. To jump in, as a novice, at the deep end will simply be too hard to cope with, physically and mentally, and you will not be able to continue for very long.

Ideal training for road racers on quiet weekends – Tour de France rider Adrian Timmis knows the benefit of mixing his racing

Principles of training

At this point let's take a look at what we are trying to achieve through physical training.

To go faster on your bike you need to produce energy at a higher rate, and energy is produced when a fuel, either carbohydrate or fat, is burned by reacting with oxygen in the muscles. The muscles receive oxygen from the blood, and the amount they get is restricted by the amount of blood the heart can pump out.

So, the two things you are trying to improve through training are the oxygen supply to the muscle and the fuel supply to the muscle.

Oxygen is supplied to the muscle from the atmosphere via the lungs and cardiovascular system, and although lung capacity doesn't change significantly through training, there is an increase in the heart's size and strength, and therefore the amount of blood transported.

To improve the oxygen transportation system you need to train at all levels from long duration/low intensity (endurance training) right through to short duration/very high intensity (interval training).

The place where all the hard work happens is the muscle. This is composed of muscle fibres which contract to produce force, and as the intensity of the exercise increases the muscle works harder by recruiting a greater proportion of its fibres into working.

A muscle fibre is only trained when it is used, and occasional bouts of very intense exercise and prolonged, moderate exercise to fatigue are needed in order to train the whole muscle.

The body's energy system is rather like your car. To make the whole thing work you need fuel, and this comes in different grades.

Carbohydrate is the 'high-octane' fuel. It can be broken down very quickly, and produces energy at a high rate, but the problem is that only limited amounts are available in the form of glycogen in the body. Glycogen is stored in the muscles and the liver, but there is only enough to last about 1½ hours into high-intensity exercise – a bit of a problem when a race lasts 2 hours!

Luckily, you have another store of fuel: fat, which you have plenty of, but which is only 'low-octane' because it cannot be broken down rapidly enough to produce energy at high rates.

The longer the duration of the training bout, the more fat there is in the fuel mixture. The fattiest fuel mixtures occur over long periods at moderate intensity, so training like this increases the body's ability to use fat as a fuel, and it becomes less reliant on using the limited stores of carbohydrate.

So, to train the oxygen transportation system, and *all* the muscle fibres to use a *choice* of fuels, you need to train at a full range of intensities from low/moderate to very high, and for a wide range of durations from one minute to three hours.

Steady-state training

If you are a novice rider just starting to race, the first thing you need to do is improve your endurance, and the best place to do this is on the road. Why the road? Well, you are looking to ride at a constant steady pace for around two hours, and the problem with riding off-road is that the pace and efforts used are not constant – one minute you are gasping up a hill, perhaps walking a while, looking at the view, freewheeling downhill: very rarely can you keep your heart-rate constant and your

pedal revs ticking over at a nice 90 rpm.

So get on your road bike, or put slicks on your mountain bike, and two or three times a week try to do 2-2½ hours of this steady-state training, which is the base for the rest of your training and which you will always need to have regardless of the level you ride at.

The four levels of training

Four basic levels of training have been established from the results of laboratory exercise tests, covering every level of intensity and duration, and by using these levels it becomes very simple to structure your training.

You can base this training on pulse rates to give you a much clearer picture of how hard you are really working. If you don't have a pulsemeter and can't afford to buy one yourself, see if you can borrow one, or buy one between a group of friends and use it on a rota. After you have used it a few times you will become accustomed to how you feel at a given heart rate and will be able to gauge what rate you are training at even when you don't have the meter.

Initially you need to obtain your threshold heart rate. This is the rate your heart beats at when you are going flat out over about 20-25 minutes: a 10-mile time trial is an excellent example.

Use the pulsemeter for a 10-mile time trial and make a mental note of your heart rate during the middle section of the ride – between 4 and 6 miles is best. This will give you a good idea of your threshold heart rate, and from this you will see how to train at the four main levels.

Level 1	Hard rides of 3-4 hours in duration: 'long, steady distance' (LSD)
Level 2	Rides of 1-1½ hours in duration
Level 3	Intense training sessions of 20-30 minutes
Level 4	Interval training – 3-minute efforts (or shorter) repeated
Recovery	Easy riding; not a training session

Level 1

Intensity Best described as a brisk pace, with breathing just at the point of becoming noticeable (deep and regular).

Heart rate Approximately threshold minus 25 beats per minute.

Duration 3-4 hours (full); 1-2 hours (short).

Frequency 1 session/week. Occasionally 2 sessions/week when time allows.

Effects Improves fuel supply, as it trains most of the fibres in a muscle to use a fatty fuel mixture, and also provides some training of the oxygen transport system.

Hints Best performed alone or in small groups. Attempt to maintain a constant pace. Correct carbohydrate feeding is important both during and immediately after training (see page 114).

Level 2

Intensity Best described as 'comfortably hard'. Breathing rate and depth are noticeably higher than at Level 1. Conversation is possible, but frequent pauses to regain breathing pattern are necessary.

Heart rate Approximately threshold minus 15 beats per minute.

Duration 1-1½ hours.

Frequency 2 sessions/week.

Effects Trains a fair proportion of the muscle fibres to use a mixture of carbohydrate and fat, and provides moderate training of the oxygen transport system.

Hints Best performed as controlled '2-up' training. Use varied terrain where possible. For any rides over 1 hour, adequate fluid and carbohydrate intake during and after training is essential.

Level 3

Intensity Very high. Virtually the same as riding a 10-mile time trial. Breathing rapid and deep. Requires intense concentration.

Heart rate Approximately threshold minus 5 beats per minute.

Duration No longer than 30 minutes.

Frequency 1 session/week.

Effects Trains most muscle fibres, and uses mainly carbohydrate for fuel. This is a high level of training

for the oxygen transport system. It accustoms the body to the physical load that will be encountered during a race.

Vary the terrain. Begin the session with a 30-minute warm-up ride, and get into the right frame of mind. Possible to ride as a '2-up' effort.

Level 4

Intensity Near maximal. Breathing very rapid and uncomfortable. Physically and psychologically very demanding.

Heart rate Heart rates are not a good guide for this type of training, as it is non-steady-state.

Duration Short intervals: 45-60 seconds. Progress to 8-10 repetitions. Long intervals: 2-3 minutes. Progress to 6 repetitions. Rest interval should be long enough to recover from the effort – around 5 minutes.

Frequency 1 session/week.

Effects Trains virtually all fibres in a muscle, and uses solely carbohydrate as a fuel. Best possible training of the oxygen transport system.

Hints Vary the terrain. Best performed alone. Warm up thoroughly.

Now you can see with each level how many times a week you need to include a certain session, and it becomes a lot simpler to draw up training plans. For instance, a typical 14 days' training could look like this:

Monday	Recovery or short Level 1
Tuesday	Level 2
Wednesday	Level 1 (3-4 hours)
Thursday	Level 3
Friday	Recovery
Saturday	Level 2
Sunday	Race
Monday	Recovery, or short Level 1
Tuesday	Level 3
Wednesday	Level 1 (3-4 hours)
Thursday	Level 4
Friday	Recovery
Saturday	Level 2
Sunday	Race

This is just an example, and you must decide yourself, or with the help of a coach, how much time you have available or are prepared to devote to training before sitting down and working out your plan.

Most people can't train full-time, and so have to fit it in around work and family commitments, so we'll have a look at how that can be done.

Training around work

It's OK for these pros, you may say – up at 9am, out at 10am for three hours, bit of lunch, watch TV, clean the bike, have a snooze and it's time for some more food!

But what about me? – up at 7am, at work by 8.30am, lucky to leave by 5pm, home at 6pm, then I've got to eat, talk to the wife, play with the children, then I'm too tired to

A bit of running in your training schedule is no bad thing: you never know what conditions you will come across during a race

train! Saturday afternoon is the only time for a ride, after the supermarket and before I mow the lawn.

Do you want to race? Do you want to improve? I guess so, otherwise you wouldn't be reading this. Well, where there's a will there's a way!

First, look at your work and the way you travel to it. Is it at all possible to leave the car at home, and commute by bike? Most people work within 10-20 miles (15-30 km) of home, or if it is less you can pad the journey out with an extra loop on the way home. You will of course need clothes to change into when you arrive at work.

Mondays and Fridays are good for resting, so travel as normal by car or public transport, and take the opportunity to bring your cycling kit home for washing and to drop off some clean clothes at work for the following week.

If you are, say, a 30-minute ride away from work, ride straight there, and increase the return trip to 1-1½ hours. In this way you can train at Levels 2, 3 and 4, only missing the LSD (long, steady distance) provided by Level 1. During the periods when you are not racing, make the most of the weekends, and try to fit in 3-hour rides on Saturday and Sunday as a minimum; or if possible try to extend Wednesday's ride home to 2-2½ hours, perhaps every other week.

If time is even tighter (how do you ever find time to ride?!), try some sessions of running. Running is great if you only have an hour-long lunch break in which to train, as you can fit a good-quality session into 20-30 minutes. If you aren't used to running, start slowly for the first couple of weeks and try to run on grass. Pay particular attention to warming up well, with a full range of stretching exercises both before and after your run; and buy the best running shoes you can afford to reduce the possibility of injuries occurring.

During the summer months, take advantage of any type of racing that is available during mid-week evenings, especially time trials, or criteriums and road races if you are a bit more experienced on the road. Time trials are great – especially those around 10 miles in length. If you don't have a road bike, ride slicks on your mountain bike, and remember you are riding them for training, not to win, so as long as you have a good hard ride your time is immaterial, although it can be a good guide to your form if you compare your times throughout the summer.

During the winter, training around work can be a real drag; dark, cold wet nights do nothing to encourage you. However, hard work really will pay dividends during the summer, and you still need to get out there and do it. Long rides at weekends are a must, and during the week you should ride for 1-1½ hours

when possible. If the weather is bad, you may prefer running, which is not so affected by cold and wet: you are moving a lot slower, so windchill is not so great, you keep really warm, and you only need 20 minutes for a good run so you are out for much less time. In addition, find a cycling club with a circuit-training evening, and get to the gym and increase your strength with a programme of weight training.

Cyclo-cross races at the weekend are also ideal for a good hard workout, and give you the chance to race off-road, thereby enabling you to practise your technique.

Here are two example schedules, which you can adapt as appropriate for your own use.

Schedule 1: Winter/off-season

Monday	Rest or weight training
Tuesday	1-1½ hours (Level 1) and circuit training
Wednesday	1½ hours (Level 2)
Thursday	1 hour (Level 2) and weight training
Friday	Rest
Saturday	2 hours (Level 1)
Sunday	Cyclo-cross or 3 hours (Level 1)

If you cannot get out in daylight during the week, try to go off-road at least once over the weekend and practise your techniques. If you can get off-road midweek, replace Tuesday or Thursday by a technique session, especially if you are a novice racer, and make

your weekend rides lengthy road ones.

If the weather is bad, or you don't have time to cycle, fit in two 20-minute runs during the week, preferably off-road.

Schedule 2: Summer/season

Monday	1 hour (Level 1)
Tuesday	10-mile time trial
Wednesday	1½ hours (Level 2) or 2 hours off-road
Thursday	2 hours (group ride if possible)
Friday	Rest
Saturday	Travel to race and practice or 2 hours steady (Level 1)
Sunday	Race

At least once a week, try to cover your race distance plus half an hour. For instance, if you race in the sports category for 1½ hours, fit in a 2-hour ride.

If you are a novice, get off-road as often as possible to practise your techniques: this will give you a lot more confidence, and will also include a good amount of training anyway. More serious training can follow when you know you can handle riding off-road with ease.

If you can still fit in one or two sessions of weight training, keep it up throughout the summer. However, if time is tight, give it a miss and go out on the bike instead.

If you can, alternate your training between road bike and mountain bike, for the sake of variety.

Training all the time on your mountain bike will leave you without the extra zip a road bike can offer. If you have only one bike, still train on-road and off-road, but use slicks on-road.

Resting around work

The most important part of a good training regime is ... resting!

The purpose of training is to place your body under physical stress over time, so it will adapt to the stresses imposed upon it and increase its ability to cope with a higher level of stress in the future. But your body needs time to adapt itself to the stress of training if it is to be of any benefit, and this comes in the form of rest.

Pros always take enough rest – when was the last time you saw a pro rushing around, or riding around the car park at a race pulling wheelies? They don't, they sit down a lot!

Unfortunately the need for rest is even greater if you work full-time, so you need to make sure it is a major part of your schedule.

If you haven't been training long, two days a week doing no training is a good idea, and Monday and Friday are best both physically and mentally. Physically it is good to have consecutive days of hard work; and mentally you can prepare for a good weekend of training after a hard week, and

make sure you are recovered on Monday before you train again on Tuesday.

Training progressively

As we have already mentioned, training must be progressive: you subject the body to stress, and, when it has adapted, you subject it again to a higher load. This is how you improve.

The best way to progress your training is by working out training 'cycles' of a number of weeks, followed by a rest week, with an increase of training intensity in the following cycle.

Cycles of 3 weeks followed by a rest week are about right for novices, 4 weeks for intermediate riders, and 5 weeks for the good guys.

During the rest week of the cycle it is important not to stop activity totally, but to do no more than what you feel like. If you are tired, don't go out; if you feel OK and the sun is shining, have a steady pedal and admire the scenery, but no training as such. Catch up on your social life, hobbies and other sports – do something active to keep ticking over, but at the same time rest enough to recover from the previous cycle and to prepare yourself mentally for the next, harder, cycle.

In this way training has some progression, and there is light at

the end of the tunnel. You know that in just two weeks, or whatever, you can have a break – you are not just training week in, week out, at the same level and going nowhere because everything is the same.

It is for the same reason that we recommend at least one day off in the week – Friday is best, even at the highest level. Thursday morning, when you are tired from the training earlier in the week, it is good to know that you've only got to train that day, and that on Friday the bike can stay at home! Of course, some weeks you will still be OK on Friday, in which case go for a nice sociable ride, but I can guarantee that sometimes you will be happy to have a day off.

Overtraining

Just as bad for you as not doing enough training is doing too much, especially too much high-intensity stuff without enough recovery.

If you get to the stage where you are training hard but your performances are going downhill, it's time to look for the other signs of overtraining.

The best indicator is your resting heart rate. Get into the habit of taking your pulse daily before you get up; if there is a variation of over 5 beats either above or below normal (usually above), you know something is not right, so take it easy.

Other signs to look out for if you are suffering from overtraining are depressed appetite, disturbed sleep and a general feeling of irritability and depression.

Chronic overtraining takes more than just a day to go away: you need a good break to recover, and then you can start building back up very slowly.

With time, athletes become highly tuned to what their bodies are telling them. It is important to realise how you are feeling all the time, and what conditions make you feel differently. In this way you can nip in the bud overuse injuries, illnesses and overtraining, which can set in and become major problems if not caught early, resulting in lost time and training while you treat them.

Stretching

As we have emphasised, one important aspect of your training routine that should never be missed is your daily dose of stretching.

You can tell the cyclists that don't stretch – they walk and hobble around as if they have just got off their bikes after a hard 100-mile ride, or have aged prematurely.

Cycling keeps your muscles in a contracted state, and your arms, legs and back do not operate through their full range of movements. It is important that this is remedied off the bike through a comprehensive routine of stretches to avoid injury, and to lessen the risk of muscular strains and soreness.

You should stretch before and after a training session or race, first thing in the morning (especially if you run then), and before bed if you feel stiff after a hard day's training.

It doesn't take long – only a matter of minutes per session – and should become routine.

Those riders we mentioned earlier, hobbling around – take a look at them on their bikes, and I'll bet they don't seem quite right. They usually look as though they are sitting too low and too far forward, riding on the front of the saddle. A lack of mobility means that they cannot pedal in the most efficient position on the bike, so they set the bike up to what feels comfortable but is in fact wrong, adding to their problems. Still, *you* stretch, *your* position is right, and you beat them anyway, so what do you care?!

Hints for effective stretching
1 Do not stretch too far. Produce a slight stretch, and hold it at that point for 20-30 seconds. The point of stretch should *never* be painful.

2 *Never* bounce. Bouncing tightens the very muscles you are trying to stretch, so stretch gently and hold it.

3 Breath slowly and deeply. Concentrate on the muscle you are stretching, and relax.

4 Never rush a set of stretches.

5 Do not try to match yesterday's efforts. You will be naturally stiffer or looser on some days than on others.

6 Do not compare yourself with others – everybody is different and has different levels of flexibility.

7 *Regular* stretching is the key. Little and often is better than a lot every now and then.

Stretching routine
This should be carried out as regularly as possible, but always before and after training, and any time you have a spare moment. Use the following as a guide, and add your own stretches as you go on. Initially, as you develop the routine, start at your head and work down. This will help you not to forget any body part.

People tend to spend more time on the first leg, arm or area they stretch, and they usually stretch their 'easy' or more flexible side first. To even out the differences in flexibility in your body, stretch your tight side first.

1 Neck roll

Very slowly roll your head around in a full circle.
5 times each direction.

2 Shoulder stretch

Interlace your fingers above your head, and with your palms upwards push your arms back and up.
15-20 seconds.

3 Triceps stretch

With your arms overhead, hold the elbow of one arm with the hand of the other arm. Gently pull the elbow behind your head.
10 seconds each arm.

4 Upper-body stretch

Stand about 18-24 inches (45-60 cm) away from a wall with your back towards it. Turn your upper body around until you can place your hands on the wall at shoulder height.
10-15 seconds for each side.

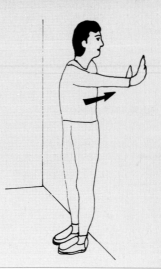

5 Lateral stretch

Stand with your feet apart and your arms at your sides. Extend one arm over your head, and slide the other arm down your leg as far as possible.
15-20 seconds each side.

6 Quad and knee stretch

Hold the top of your right foot with your left hand, and gently pull your heel towards your buttocks. (The knee bends at a natural angle when you hold your foot with the opposite hand.)
30 seconds each leg.

7 Hamstring stretch

Place your feet wide apart. With your legs straight, slide both hands down the front of one leg until you feel the stretch down the back of your hamstring.
15-20 seconds each leg.

8 Hamstring stretch

Place the back of your heel on a table or other solid object around waist height. Keeping both legs straight, lean forward at the waist until you feel the stretch down the back of the raised leg.
20-30 seconds each leg.

9 Adductor stretch

Stretch one leg out sideways, and bend the other knee. With one hand on that knee, transfer your weight to the bent leg, and feel the stretch along the inside of your thigh.
15-20 seconds each leg.

10 Spinal twist

Sit with your right leg straight. Bend your left leg, cross your left foot over, and rest it on the outside of your right knee. Then bend your right elbow and rest it on the outside of your upper left thigh, just above the knee. With your left hand resting behind you, turn your head to look over your left shoulder.
20-25 seconds each side.

11 Calf stretch

Stand a little way from a wall, and lean on it with your forearms. Bend one leg in front of you, and keep the back leg straight. Move your hips forward and feel the stretch up the back of the calf. Be sure to keep your heel on the floor.
30 seconds each leg.

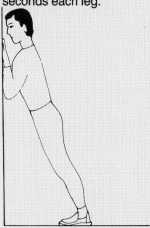

12 Lower calf/Achilles stretch

From the position described in **11** above, slightly bend the knee on the straight leg, and keep the heel on the ground. Feel the stretch move down your calf to your achilles tendon.
30 seconds each leg.

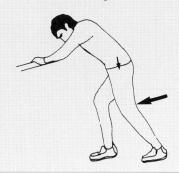

Weight training

Weight training for mountain bikers is an important part of their schedule, as it is the best way to isolate and strengthen certain muscles that fatigue quickly. These muscles are not worked in isolation when cycling, but as a group, and will not strengthen significantly as a result of cycling only. The best examples are your forearms, upper arms and shoulders, which always ache as much as your legs after a race, and which are in use continually for climbing and descending.

Decide for yourself how much weight training you need. For instance, if you have a heavy manual job you will probably not need to strengthen your arms and shoulders, but if you sit at a desk all day you almost certainly will.

Nowadays it is not necessary to use free weights; the technology of multi-gyms means that any muscle can be worked on a machine without the risk of injury from the inexperienced use of free weights.

Leg adductor machine (inner thigh)

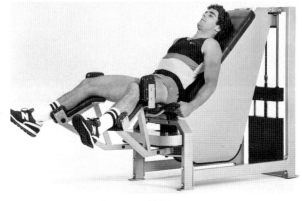

Leg abduction machine (outer thigh)

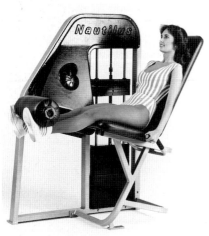

Leg extension quads)

Bicep/tricep pulldown

Legcurl (hamstring)

The big battles for supremacy continue between 1990 World Champion Juli Furtado and multi-titled Alison Sydor

Work out a weight-training programme with the aid of an experienced person, such as an instructor in the gym. Explain what it is you do and what you are trying to achieve, and the instructor will plan a programme to include all the appropriate body parts. All the exercises will be performed to increase the muscular endurance of each body part, so you will perform a high number of repetitions at a relatively low weight. Muscular power, developed by using heavy weights with few repetitions, is not for you. You are not looking to become a bodybuilder on a bike!

You should try to fit in a session of weights at least twice a week, three times if possible for the best effect, and continue throughout the season. If after a race you notice that one body part is more tired or aching more than any other, then concentrate on building up the strength of that part.

One useful addition to the weight programme is the use of a hand/wrist strengthener to avoid the pain and fatigue caused by long bumpy descents. These can be bought quite cheaply from sports shops and consist of a sprung piece of metal which you squeeze repeatedly. You can use it

Skier turned mountain bike racer, Mike Kloser has improved his performance each year to match the high levels of fitness shown by the influx of road and cyclo-cross stars. He has become one of the most respected riders on the World Cup circuit

at any time, even in front of the television! (Squeezing a tennis ball has the same effect.)

Weight training must be *progressive* for it to work. Don't perform the same exercises week in, week out, at the same weight and same number of repetitions.

Start at a comfortable weight, at which you can perform 3 sets of 15 repetitions. Then do 2 sets of 15 reps and 1 of 20, then 1 of 15 and 2 of 20, then 3 of 20. When you can do that, increase the weight and drop back to 3 of 15 reps.

If you cannot manage 15 reps of an exercise, the weight is too heavy, so reduce it. Don't worry – your strength will increase quite quickly in the early stages, and you won't be using the lightest weights for long!

Weight-training exercises
Use the following exercises as the basis for your programme, and add your own, depending on what machines are available in the gym and what your instructor advises.

Always start with a thorough warm-up consisting of your stretching routine followed by 5 minutes on a static exercise bike or a treadmill.

Similarly afterwards, have a gentle pedal on the static bike to warm down, and gently stretch any muscles that feel tight.

1 Inner thigh
2 Outer thigh
3 Leg extensions, single
4 Leg curls, single or double
5 Calf raises

6 Bench press, lying or seated
7 Pulldowns, standing or sitting
8 Lateral raises
9 Triceps pushdown
10 Upright rowing

In addition to the above, you can supplement your programme with:

11 Sit-ups
12 Back hyperextensions
13 Chins
14 Hanging leg raises, which don't require the use of weights

Circuit training

If circuit training is available to you, by all means take advantage of it, especially during the winter. A lot of cycling and football clubs have a weekly session then for their members, which you could join in.

Circuit training consists of a number of exercises in a gym, some using apparatus and some not. Warm up first, then do each in turn, usually for a minute, during which time you attempt to do as many repetitions of the exercise as possible. After a brief rest you move on to the next exercise, and so on, for about ten or twelve exercises. The complete circuit is then repeated.

This type of training is best performed in pairs. One partner can time and count as the other performs, and vice versa, giving equal times of effort and recovery – and you can compare your scores.

9 High-level training

Hopefully you will reach the stage when you have more time available to train, and decide to aim for a bit more success, perhaps to move up a class. Maybe you've had reasonable success at intermediate level on only part-time training, and you are curious to see how you could do against the pros with some more training. However you end up there, you need to train like a pro – but how?

A word of warning: don't jump in at the deep end. If you are working and training eight hours a week, don't suddenly double it – it will be too hard! *Gradually* increase the schedule, not forgetting the rest phases, until you are accustomed to the stresses involved.

This warning is especially important for riders in the youngest age groups (Juvenile and Junior), who shouldn't attempt any high-level training plans until they are older, unless they are being supervised by a responsible coach.

Practice is as important as physical training for downhill racers

For any rider entering a higher-level phase of training, it is a good idea to find a coach, or at least someone you can sit down with and discuss how you feel and what you think you should be doing. Qualified coaches don't really exist in mountain bike racing as they do in other branches of cycling, but there are plenty of people around who can help you out and provide a friendly ear when things aren't going right.

The racing year can be split into three: off-season, preparation phase and racing season.

Off-season

December–mid-February (11 weeks)

Following your break after the previous season, your preparation for the following year starts at the beginning of December, and the gradual build-up should include a good variety of exercise to improve your general strength and cardiovascular fitness.

Daily stretching should become part of your life. Develop a range of stretching exercises (see page 104), and add others of your own

as you go along. During this period you will be cycling, running, weight training and perhaps skiing if it is available, so keeping supple and well stretched is vital if you are to keep injury-free. Indeed, this applies not only at this time of year but also during the race season.

If you are in an area where cyclo-cross races are available to you, make the most of them – they provide excellent competitive training. Don't forget that virtually all of Europe's top mountain bike racers come from a cyclo-cross background and owe a lot of their fitness and skill to it. It promotes excellent bike handling, and gives you an intense hour of effort that is simply not available in training unless you are super-motivated to do interval training extensively, which not many people are!

Miles on the bike are best done on the road, keeping at a steady, regular pace and cadence. Anyway, off-road riding at this time of year is usually very messy – save getting dirty for the cyclo-cross races. These rides should be social, with no pressure, and are best done in a group to keep them interesting.

111

Weight training and circuit training should start now, and the weight training should be kept up throughout the summer if possible. Similarly, running begins now to keep your heart and lungs in shape; start off steadily and off-road, as supple cycling muscles don't react well to pounding on pavements.

Split this initial 11-week phase into two cycles with a rest week in the middle, and increase the training during the second cycle.

Here is a typical weekly schedule for the first cycle:

Monday	1 hour steady, plus weights
Tuesday	Run (20 mins) plus 2-3 hours on-road
Wednesday	Run (20 mins) plus 2 hours off-road plus weights
Thursday	Run (20 mins) plus 2-3 hours on-road
Friday	Rest *or* 1 hour steady or weights
Saturday	2 hours steady
Sunday	Cyclo-cross *or* 3-4 hours on-road

Most of this on-road training is at Level 1, but throw in the occasional Level 2 session, especially if you are not doing any cyclo-cross races.

And don't forget the stretching!

Preparation phase

Mid-February – mid-April (8 weeks)

After a steady week at the end of the off-season phase, you will be ready to go into the next phase, which will take you up to your first races during April. You will notice that the quantity has gone up, although the quality remains about the same. However, some more off-road riding is included to accustom your arms, shoulders and hands to the battering they get, and this will automatically increase the quality of some sessions, as the efforts off-road are a lot less regular than on the road, and usually the terrain forces you to make harder efforts.

If you are not happy running you can drop it now, but if you enjoy running it is worth doing it, say, twice a week to supplement your work on the bike.

Now is also the time to start sorting out your equipment and getting used to any new items – especially different frames – or new components. There's no need to use them all the time and wear them out, but do accustom yourself to how any new equipment handles and works before you need to race on it.

Again, split this 8-week stint into a 3-week cycle and a 4-week one with a rest week in between, and increase the training intensity for the second cycle. And don't forget the stretching!

Here is a typical weekly schedule for the first cycle:

Monday	2 hours steady on-road
Tuesday	2 hours on-road, plus weights
Wednesday	4 hours off-road
Thursday	3 hours medium on-road, plus weights
Friday	Rest *or* 1 hour steady
Saturday	4-6 hours on – or off-road
Sunday	4-6 hours opposite to Saturday

Racing season

Mid-April – September (22 weeks)

This is the important stuff – the racing. The quantity goes down a little bit, but the quality goes up, with more Level 2 and 3 sessions. Try to fit in some criteriums or road races to keep you sharp and stop yourself losing interest with just mountain bike racing every weekend.

Monday	2 hours steady on-road, plus weights
Tuesday	1½ hours on-road and 2 hours off-road
Wednesday	2 hours on-road, plus weights
Thursday	4 hours off-road
Friday	Rest *or* 1 hour steady
Saturday	Travel to race and course inspection/training
Sunday	Race

Split this phase into four cycles as follows:

- 4-week cycle
- rest week
- 5-week cycle
- rest week
- 5-week cycle
- rest week
- 4-week cycle, leading up to ...
- ... the World Championships.

Make each cycle progressively harder, and swap some Level 2 for Level 3 as you get into August and September.

Peaking for big races

There is no magic to peaking for a major event: it is down to good preparation and getting the right frame of mind. You will need to train through some lesser races, and must accept that the results will not be as good as they could be – no matter, these races are a means to an end.

Firstly, find out about the big race – its length, course details, expected weather, etc – and tailor your training around it. If it contains steep single-track climbs, go and find some similar ones. If there are likely to be some running sections, include some more running in your schedule.

Plan your other races around the major one – don't have a heavy race the weekend before if it can be avoided, but ride a small race and train through it – don't rest Friday and Monday as normal, but ease off instead from the Tuesday or Wednesday before the 'big one'. Spend that week focusing on what you are about to do, and get your equipment into the best possible condition. Increase your rest and your intake of carbohydrate, and above all, don't overtrain in a panic – if you haven't done it by now, it's too late!

10 Nutrition for racing

Remember the section on 'Principles of training', and its emphasis on the fuel store in the body (see page 97)? Well, like any fuel it needs to be supplied, and in the case of a hard-working cyclist this is done via the mouth in the form of food.

No matter how hard you train, how shiny your bike is, or how great is your will to win, if you don't feed the 'engine' with the best quality fuel there is no possible way you can perform at your best.

Nutrients

The food you eat contains the following nutrients: carbohydrate, fat and protein. It also contains vitamins, minerals, trace elements, dietary fibre and water.

No one food contains enough of each of these to meet the needs of the body fully: hence the need for a 'balanced diet'.

The standard Western diet is good enough to ensure that you do in fact get adequate supplies of all the above – and, in the case of fats, significantly too much. However, you are not a standard Western person – you are a mountain bike racer – so you need a bit more of certain things to cope with the raised levels of energy you have to produce.

The most important nutrient to you as a racer is *carbohydrate.* Carbohydrates come in two forms: complex (starches) and simple (sugars). The best for you are the complex carbohydrates, obtained from foods such as potatoes, bread, pasta, pulses, vegetables and nuts. In addition to the starch within these foods, there are also all the vitamins and minerals that are necessary to metabolise the carbohydrate.

Simple carbohydrates are usually found in highly processed foods where the carbohydrate has been extracted from the natural sources and broken down: confectionery and sweet foods and drinks are usually high in simple carbs, and contain 'empty calories' – energy but nothing else.

Fat is used as the 'low-octane' fuel when riding, and is needed extensively as a fuel source, especially on long rides, but this does not mean that you need a high intake of fat. As already stated, the Western diet is too high in fat, so you should eat as little fatty food as possible; your body will get all it needs from hidden fats in other foods.

Protein is another source of energy, as well as being required to manufacture and repair muscle. The best sources are white meat, fish, beans, pulses, legumes, nuts and (skimmed) milk.

Carbohydrate supplements

But back to carbohydrates: tests have shown that you need to have very large amounts of carbohydrates during training and racing to fuel the energy being expended. These amounts cannot be provided by food intake alone – the bulk would simply be too much – so you must use carbo-rich drinks to supplement your food intake during and after training and racing.

The recommended quantities of carbohydrate intake are as follows:

Training	½ g carbohydrate/kg body weight/hour
Racing	1 g carbohydrate/kg body weight/hour
Refuelling	1½ g carbohydrate/kg body weight

This means, for example, that a 60 kg person needs to consume 30 g carbs an hour in training, 60 g an hour during a race, and 90 g of carbs as soon as possible after racing when the body is most receptive to refuelling. Now you could try to take this amount in the form of food, but a slice of bread provides only about 10 g of carbs, and eating six slices of bread an hour on your bike is not going to be too practical. So taking the carbs in liquid form is much better – you have a bottle on your bike, and can re-hydrate as well as feed at the same time.

The ideal carbohydrate drink mix is a pure complex carbohydrate prepared from corn starch. It is flavourless and contains no sugars or salts to cause stomach upsets, and very concentrated solutions can be made and digested without problems.

Work out (as above) how many grams of carbohydrate you will need during the race. Next decide how many bottles you will drink: if it is cold perhaps just one, or up to five if it is a hot day. Then simply divide the amount evenly into however many bottles you decide on. If you eat something as well during a race, then take that into consideration: for example, a Powerbar, which is the most popular source of energy during a race, contains 40 g carbohydrate.

You can only use these high concentrations of drink mix if it is pure and unflavoured, such as Carboplex and Maxim. Drinks such as Gatorade, Dynacarb and Isostar must never be used in a concentration higher than that recommended by the manufacturer, as gastric emptying is impaired and a stomach upset will result. If you use these drinks, check the amount of carbohydrate you are getting from the recommended number of scoops per bottle, and either drink more bottles or supplement them with Powerbars!

Riders who have stuck to the above guidelines for carbohydrate feeding during racing and training have noticed great improvements in their ability to recover faster after a hard race. They can also train hard on successive days without the previous feeling of tiredness. The results of better training and recovery are obvious – better racing performance!

Vitamin supplements

Nutritionists tell us that a normal diet provides enough of all the vitamins and minerals we require, and that vitamin supplements are a waste of money as you simply flush them away. However, they are so cheap that I think it is worth taking a vitamin/mineral supplement once a day just to make sure, and an iron supplement is also a good move, especially for women.

A daily supplement keeps your levels topped up, and will not contain high enough amounts of fat-soluble vitamins to cause you any problems. Take care, though: don't think that because a vitamin is good for you, a megadose is very good for you. Large doses of vitamins or minerals can be harmful.

Daily diet

Most people, especially athletes, are a lot more aware of what they eat now compared with, say, 10 years ago, and the basic guidelines for a healthy diet should be obvious to everyone. Reduce your fat intake, reduce sugar intake (including confectionery), increase complex-carbohydrate intake, and eat as much fresh, raw, unrefined vegetables and fruit as possible.

Reliance on 'junk' food and 'fast' food is usually the result of bad preparation or time management. Actually it takes no longer to cook a bowl of pasta than it does to fry a steak, but you are probably more used to the latter – try to change your ways!

Breakfast is easy – muesli, wholemeal toast, orange juice, fruit, yoghurt are all quick, easy and full of the right things. At midday, wholemeal bread sandwiches with a low-fat filling are quick and nutritious. In the evening, pasta, baked potatoes, fresh vegetables, white meat or fish are again quick, easy and no problem to even the worst cooks! Between meals, eat fruit, muesli bars or Powerbars, and replace fizzy drinks with fresh fruit juice or plain water.

Don't worry about the occasional lapses – the odd hamburger or curry is not going to do you any harm, just don't live on them every day.

Pre-race eating

We have already covered pre-race food under 'Race routine' (see page 55), but here is a summary to remind you:

Don't eat anything within the last two hours before you race or train. In training this will cause your body to adapt to using fat as a fuel, saving your stores of glycogen. Ideally, try to have your pre-race meal three hours before you start. This should be high in carbs, low in fat and easily digestible. Pasta is the racer's favourite, with perhaps cheese, ham and tomato sauce to make it more interesting, but if you have to eat early and can't face pasta, eat toast, cereal and fruit instead.

Alex Balaud wrestles with the course at Metabief, France 1994

11 Staying healthy

Keeping clear of injury and remaining healthy throughout the season is hard, but worth working at, as you cannot afford to lose time recovering from something when ideally you should be training. Niggling little twinges can go away – or they can become niggling big twinges that need treatment. Colds can clear up in three days, or they can lead to chest or sinus infections that require antibiotics to shift them. This is partly up to you, as you can take common-sense steps yourself to limit the time lost through these things.

In time you will come to understand your body better, including the effects training has on it, and will be more finely tuned to pick up the signs of when it is not running smoothly.

By checking your pulse regularly, you will be able to spot signs of overtraining (see page 102) or of the onset of illness, and by taking more care of yourself at the early stages you will have more chance of limiting the effects.

Get into the habit of changing out of your training kit as soon as you get home. Even more important, don't lie around after a race without changing your jersey or putting another layer on top. Even when the weather is good, wet clothing cools fast and causes a big drop in body temperature.

Away from the race, look after your eyes, and get all the dust and grit out with an eye bath. Treat any saddle soreness problems immediately, as infection can easily start in hair follicles, causing saddle boils which will certainly keep you off your bike.

Regular anti-tetanus injections are a must, and visits to the dentist should be for check-ups, not just when you need treatment. Even something so simple as a decaying tooth can affect your form, so make sure your teeth are healthy.

Injury

Injury can occur in a number of ways – often as a result of a fall, or through overuse of a body part.

Falls are, alas, unavoidable. Forget what you may have read about learning to fall – nine times out of ten, one minute you are riding along, the next minute you're on the floor, and there isn't much time to execute a tuck and roll! By regular stretching you will be more flexible and will not be as liable to straining something when you fall.

Similarly with overuse injuries: tight muscles, especially between the knee and the thigh, cause imbalances, and knee problems result. Something simple like a stiff shoulder can affect the way you sit on your bike. Then you try to compensate for it, which leads to lower-back pain, and even to referred pain down a leg. The message is simple – stay supple!

If injury does occur, act immediately to help the healing process. The standard procedure is **RICE** (Rest, Ice, Compression, Elevation). This helps to reduce swelling and restricts the spread of bruising, both of which can delay healing. The first six hours after an injury are the most important, so apply ice (never heat), bandage and elevate the affected limb, and get expert treatment as soon as possible.

Never rush back into training after injury or illness: start steadily, ensure that all the symptoms have gone, and *gradually* build up to the level you were at before the enforced lay-off.

Massage

If massage is available, use it – massage can help you recover a lot faster from a hard race or training. If you can't get a massage easily, self-massage is worth the effort, and you don't have to rely on anybody else. Start in a sitting position – in the bath is ideal – and begin at your ankles and work upwards. First will be the calf muscles between your ankle and knee. Use steady stroking movements upwards, towards the heart, and apply firm pressure. Next do the hamstrings at the back of the thigh, and finish with the quadriceps at the front.

Don't think that because you have a massage you don't need to stretch as much – the two complement each other well, but don't replace each other.

A picturesque Italian piazza is the setting for the start of a World Cup *event*

Some great riders

Sara Ballantyne (USA)

The queen of mountain bike racing. Until the 1990 Worlds in Durango, Sara had dominated women's off-road racing in the States and Europe for three years. She won the Mammoth Worlds three years running, two European World titles, and basing herself in Europe in 1990 she took the Grundig World Cup Series, repeating the feat in 1991 with a last round second place which snatched the title from series leader Juli Furtado.

A lot of her tough qualities can be attributed to her winter pastime, climbing, when she leaves the bike at home and scales the heights of mountains such as the Eiger and Mount McKinley.

Sara Ballantyne long dominated women's racing, finally being toppled by Furtado in the 1990 World Championships

Thomas Frischknecht
(Switzerland)

Although still only in his early twenties, Thomas is proving the man to beat in any off-road race, whether mountain bike or cyclo-cross. World junior cyclo-cross champion in 1988, he turned senior and gained a bronze in the Amateur Championships in 1990, the same year he finished second to Overend in the mountain bike 'Worlds'. 1991 saw him take the cyclo-cross title in the Netherlands and a second silver medal in the World Mountain Bike Championships in Italy – in front of Overend this time, but behind his American compatriot Tomac. He will surely add to his collection of rainbow jerseys with the mountain bike title before long. Seemingly without any weaknesses, he proved at Durango that he can handle tough circuits and altitude, but he is also happy on flat, fast circuits. He became only the second European to win a NORBA race when he won at Mount Snow, Vermont, in 1990.

Swiss star Thomas Frischknecht excels at off-road racing: within six months he became World Cyclo-cross Champion and runner-up in the world Mountain Bike Championships

Silvia Fürst (Switzerland)

It is only right that top-flight mountain bike racers should emerge from such ideal terrain as Switzerland's impressive mountains, and in Silvia Fürst the Swiss have a determined and consistent rider. Over the three years of the Grundig World Cup she can claim an overall victory from her numerous top three placings, including beating Sara Ballantyne and winning a European Championship title.

Her finest ride to date was her great third place in the 1991 World Championships on the tough Italian circuit at Il Ciocco, where she battled with Swiss team-mate Chantal Daucourt before pulling clear for her first Worlds medal.

Juli Furtado (USA)

A relative newcomer to top-flight mountain biking, it certainly didn't taken Juli long to reach the top with an emphatic victory in the Worlds at Durango, beating the more established superstar Sara Ballantyne into second place. 1991 saw her start her season superbly in Europe, taking both opening rounds of the World Cup, but her form deserted her when it mattered most; she lost the blue World Cup leader's jersey in the final round and crashed out of the World Championships.

Swiss Silvia Fürst was amongst the first of the top European women to break into the leading ranks currently dominated by the Americans

A relative newcomer to off-road racing, ex-skiier, ex-roadie Juli Furtado won the 1990 Women's World Championship at her first attempt

Henrik Djernis (Denmark)

The Danes have a long tradition of success in cycle sport and can now boast several world-class riders. Their leading exponent is Henrik Djernis, a former cyclo-cross world champion who has made the MTB World Championship his own, scoring an unprecedented tally of wins since 1992. Victory was his regardless of terrain, from the dry dusty slopes of Bromont in Canada to the treacherous mud of Métabief, France. Climbing the soaring altitude of Vail, Colorado proved him a rider of immense all-round ability. Along with his world championship successes he has had world cup wins in Germany, Great Britain and Belgium, making Henrik one of the most respected riders on the international circuit.

Tim Gould (Great Britain)

Tim was the first European to take on the Americans at their own game – and win! Tim shocked America by winning the NORBA finals at Big Bear in 1989, and rubbed salt in their wounds by doing it on a French bike with Italian components.

He first came to prominence as a mountain bike racer by coming third at the European Worlds in Crans Montana in 1988 behind Kloser and Overend, and with his team-mate, David Baker, he continued to dominate racing in Europe. In true European style, Tim comes from a cyclo-cross background, with top ten World Championship placings both as a junior and senior, and with six wins and a course record in the famous Three Peaks cyclo-cross in the North of England. Following his third place in the Worlds at

Tim Gould, the first European rider to take on the Americans on their home ground and win

Purgatory, Durango, Gould took to the road in the two-week Tour of Mexico to show his huge all-round abilities.

Happiest when the ground goes up, Tim can point to two World Uphill titles in 1989 and 1990 as proof that he is currently the best climber in the world. His ambition? The rainbow jersey − and with the next two Worlds at lower elevations you could do worse than put your money on this man!

Rishi Grewal (USA)

Another brilliant performer on- or off-road, Rishi won the USA National Road title in 1989, and finished second twice in the Mammoth Worlds in 1988 and 1989, behind Overend and Myrah respectively. Mammoth is his favourite hunting ground, but the big win there has always eluded him, except on the road where he has won the Mammoth stage race.

One of the band of Americans who have travelled to Europe to compete in the big races, Rishi aspires to a high World Cup placing before turning his attention to selection for the 1992 Olympic Road Team.

Greg Herbold (USA)

The downhill king, Herbold mastered the difficult Durango downhill course to take the first

One of the men on form in 1991 − Rishi Grewal − winner of the NORBA and World Cup races and the inaugural Ride of your life *televised spectacular in Vail, Colorado*

rainbow jersey ever awarded for a mountain bike race, proving that the descending skills that had already claimed him two wins in NORBA downhills in 1990 were in fact the best in the world. A complete equipment freak, Herbold is the ultimate test rider for component manufacturers to test their products on – no one else (except perhaps Tomac) can put equipment under quite as much pressure, and this has led to many lucrative endorsement contracts from companies who can make the most of his flamboyant image.

Mike Kloser (USA)

The original nice guy! Mike based himself in Europe following his win at the Euro Worlds in Switzerland in 1988, and his affable nature and gutsy riding have proved popular wherever he races.

Keen to lose his 'eternal second' tag awarded after his two second places in the Grundig series in Europe and in the World Downhill Championship in Durango, he wants to prove his ability with a win in the World Cup series.

His background in skiing makes him fearless downhill, and on top form he can climb with the best, making him a true all-rounder.

World downhill champion Greg Herbold – what comes down must go up!

Top of all the popularity polls, American Mike Kloser has based himself in Europe with great success

Mike Kluge made the transition from cyclo-cross to win the 1990 World Cup Series in Europe

Mike Kluge (Germany)

Kluge came from a road and 'cross background to win the Grundig World Cup Series at his first attempt in 1990, but was unable to hold his blistering early-season form until the time it mattered, and was a non-starter in Durango. Twice a World Cyclo-cross Champion on the icy courses of Munich and Mlada Boleslav in 1986 and 1987, Mike decided mud and cold were not for him, and moved into the lucrative six-day circuit held on steeply banked tracks in stadiums around Europe. He is equally adept on the road, with stage wins in the Peace Race and the Grand Prix William Tell. If he puts his mind to it he can be successful, but he has trouble holding his form throughout the season. He would love to prove his detractors wrong by carrying off a world title, and has the ability if he can get himself mentally prepared.

Ned Overend (USA)

The undisputed king of mountain bike racing, Ned won the 1990 inaugural UCI World Championship in Purgatory, part of his home town of Durango, to become the first wearer of the rainbow jersey. At 36 years old Ned has the experience to prepare for selected events; he does this with amazing consistency, as witness his five NORBA National Championship wins and two unofficial World Championship titles at Mammoth. He excels at high altitude and on tough climbing circuits.

King Ned

Regina Steifl (Germany)

Currently one of the best of the European women, Regina has stepped out of the shadow of her younger sister, Susi Buchweiser, to emerge as one of the strongest Euro challengers to the American domination of women's racing. Third places behind Furtado and Ballantyne in European races at the beginning of 1991 showed that the gap is being reduced, and if Regina's sister Susi makes a comeback with the form with which she finished 1990, the battle between the two of them could lessen it even further.

John Tomac (USA)

The best known and best paid mountain bike racer in the world, and following his storming win in the '91 Worlds cross-country in Italy, proud owner of the rainbow jersey. Second in the previous day's downhill, Tomac was never overtaken in the cross-country, erasing the downhill disappointment and setting himself up for even more fame and fortune.

Tomac won the European version of the world championships in 1989 before turning his hand to professional road racing with the powerful 7-Eleven squad in 1990 and Motorola in 1991. Although his off-road excursions were few, he

Germany's Regina Steifl − one of the Europeans leading the challenge to the Americans

still managed Norba and Grundig wins and was placed sixth in the '90 World Championships on home ground despite a puncture.

It's hard to open a mountain bike magazine without seeing John endorsing products from handlebar grips to roof racks, and his outrageous use of dropped bars and disc wheels on his mountain bike keeps him firmly in front of the camera whenever he rides.

Classic races

Races come and go, in much the same way as riders, but some are here to stay and in the short life of mountain bike racing have become classics.

Until 1991 America had its NORBA series and Europe its Grundig series, with very little crossover between the two. Mike Kloser and Sara Ballantyne became Euroyanks, as much to satisfy sponsors' requirements as for personal gain, and Tim Gould turned up at a NORBA final the week before the Worlds in Mammoth, but apart from that the two continents kept themselves very much to themselves. Then the World Cup became officially recognised by the UCI – the

John Tomac – the cult hero of mountain bike racers everywhere

controlling body of world cycling — and hey presto, the two came together to stage a nine-race series.

For some reason the classic European courses were not selected for World Cup status, being kept instead for a small, Europe-only, Grundig Challenge series, but America obliged by giving World Cup status to three of the existing NORBA venues at Mammoth, Park City and Travers City.

Of these, Mammoth stands out as the classic American venue. The World Championship course for three years from 1987 until 1989, and selected as the NORBA finals venue in 1990, no doubt Mammoth will see the UCI Worlds before long. Located in California some 300 miles (500km) north of Los Angeles, the course rises to over 11,000 feet (3350m) at the summit of Mammoth Mountain, from where racers in the famous Kamikaze downhill launch themselves for around seven minutes of breathtaking descent at speeds of over 50mph (80km/h)!

Park City, Utah has a history of silver mining, and more recently has developed a fine ski area which of course makes it ideally suited to mountain biking. Another high altitude course, with a base level of over 7000 feet (2100m), the predominantly single-track circuit

Don Myra, 1989 World Champion

saw Dave Wiens score his first NORBA victory in 1990.

Traverse City is in the lowlands, among the lakes on Michigan's lower peninsula, and the rolling sandy circuit will favour the European 'cross riders, with their technical skills and preference for lower altitude! Also a favourite on the course is local lad John Tomac, winner of the NORBA race here in 1990.

Other classic venues in the United States include Big Bear Lake in California; Durango, the venue for the World Championships in 1990; and Mount Snow in South Vermont.

Moving to Europe, the established venues are fewer, as everyone is competing to keep dates and venues fixed, but a few such as the downhill course in Kaprun, Austria, and the impressive Holmenkollen ski-jump area outside Oslo in Norway prove popular with riders and crowds alike. In Britain the Aviemore classic in Scotland looks threatened by protests from rambling organisations, but the Man v Horse and Malvern classics attract thousands of entries and look set to continue well into the nineties, as do races such as the Roc d'Azur on the Mediterranean coast of France.

World Championship results

1993 Metabief, France

Men's cross-country
1 Henrik Djernis, Denmark
2 Marcel Gerritsen, Netherlands
3 Jan Ostergaard, Denmark
4 Marcel Arntz, Netherlands
5 Albert Iten, Switzerland
6 Roger Honneger, Switzerland
7 Gerhardt Zadrobilek, Austria
8 Jan Wiejak, Poland
9 David Huarez, USA
10 Barrie Clarke, Raleigh

Women's cross-country
1 Paolo Pezzo, Italy
2 Jeannie Longo-Ciprelli, France
3 Ruthie Matthes, USA
4 Alison Sydor, Canada
5 Sophie Eglin, France
6 Nathalie Fiat, France
7 Teresa Williams, USA
8 Lisa Muhich, USA
9 Susan DeMattei, USA
10 Hedda Zu Putlitz, Germany

Junior men's cross-country
1 Dario Aquaroli, Italy
2 Gerben De Knegt, Netherlands
3 Klaus Jakobsmeier, Germany
4 Filippo Belloni, Italy
5 Dennis Hummelsiep, Germany
6 Johan Van De Ven, Netherlands
7 Miguel Martinez, France
8 Ray Donath, Germany
9 Georg Hechenblaikner, Austria
10 Matthew Guy, Great Britain

Veteran men's cross-country
1 Riccardo De Bertolis, Italy
2 Zbigniew Krasniak, France
3 Yves Berlioux, France
4 Erich Ubelhardt, Switzerland
5 Mario Norris, Italy
6 Siefried Hohenwarter, Austria
7 Alain Daniel, France
8 Walter Brändli, Switzerland
9 Uli Rottler, Germany
10 Jacques Desportes, France

Veteran women's cross-country
1 Maria Cannins, Italy
2 Dany Bonnoront, France
3 Pat Hadley, USA
4 Kari DiSteffano, USA
5 Irene Kokotailo, Canada
6 Edie Fisher, Canada
7 Claire Osbourne, Great Britain
8 Jennifer Kun, USA
9 M-Josee Brumachon, France
10 Francoise Gabilet, France

Men's downhill
1 Mike King, USA
2 Paolo Caramellino, Italy
3 Myles Rockwell, USA
4 Bruno Zanchi, Italy
5 Corrado Herrin, Italy
6 Franck Roman, France
7 Dave Cullinan, USA
8 Jurgen Beneke, Germany
9 Francois Gachet, France
10 Jurgen Sprich, Germany

Greg Herbold

Women's downhill
1 Giovanna Bonazzi, Italy
2 Kim Sonier, USA
3 Missy Giove, USA
4 Leigh Donovan, USA
5 Penny Davidson, USA
6 Eladee Brown, Canada
7 Sophie Kempf, France
8 Linda Spiazzi, Italy
9 Cindy Devine, Canada
10 Leslie Osmundsen, USA

Junior men's downhill
1 Nicolas Vouilloz, France
2 Markus Klausman, Germany
3 Karim Amour, France
4 Ivan Oulego-Moreno, Spain
5 Morten Jemtegaard, Norway
6 Cedric Gracia, France
7 Thomas Damiani, Italy
8 Florent Poussin, France
9 Gregory Noce, France
10 Dario Zampieri, Italy

Veteran men's downhill
1 Walter Brändli, Switzerland
2 Claudio Riverditi, Italy
3 Lorenzo Orlando, Italy
4 Mario Bianchi, Italy
5 Kevin Holder, USA
6 Giuseppi Lochi, Italy
7 Carlo Mazzucato, Italy
8 Isao Ida, Japan
9 Roland Champion, Switzerland
10 Marc Namur, Germany

Junior women's downhill
1 Anne-Caroline Chausson, France
2 Nolven LeCaer, France
3 Helen Mortimer, Great Britain
4 Mona Fee, France
5 Laetitia Holweck, France
6 Carole Grange, France
7 Keeley Lockey, Great Britain
8 Ines Rodriguez, Spain
9 Melanie Eberle, Germany
10 Christine Probst, Switzerland

John Tomac

1994 Vail, USA

Men's cross-country
1 Henrik Djernis, Denmark
2 Tinker Juarez, USA
3 Bart Brentjens, Netherlands
4 Daniele Pontoni, Italy
5 Daniele Bruschi, Italy
6 Paul Willertin, USA
7 Lennie Kristensen, Denmark
8 Michael Rasmussen, Denmark
9 Jean-Christophe Savignoni, France
10 Andres Brenes,COS

Women's cross-country
1 Alison Sydor, Canada
2 Susan DeMattei, USA
3 Sara Ballantyne, USA
4 Jeannie Longo, France
5 Ruthie Matthes, USA
6 Juli Furtado, USA
7 Maria Turcutto, Italy
8 Eva Orvosova, SLO
9 Jill Smith, Canada
10 Caroline Alexander, Great Britain

Junior men's cross-country
1 Miguel Martinez, France
2 Cadel Evans, Austria
3 Thomas Hochstrasser, Switzerland
4 Thomas Kalberer, Switzerland
5 Gene Hilton, USA
6 Marco Rocchi, Italy
7 Charles Heaton, USA
8 Eric Jungaker, Sweden
9 Mathias Wanner, Switzerland
10 Rodrigo Luiz-Martinez, Spain

Tim Gould

Junior women's cross-country
1 Karin Romer, Germany
2 Mona Fee, France
3 Nicole Peitzmeier, Germany
4 Adriana Santos Nasciemento, Brazil
5 Marielle Saner, Switzerland
6 Rachel Pickett, Great Britain
7 Willow Korber, USA
8 Nolven LeCaer, France
9 Emanuella Bouttecon, France
10 Nadege Garcia, France

Veteran men's cross-country
1 Riccardo DeBertolis, Italy
2 Siegfried Hochenwarter, Austria
3 Marcel Russenberger, Switzerland
4 Mario Norris, Italy
5 Sylvain Oskwarek, France
6 Zibigniew Krasniak, France
7 Silvano Ianes, Italy
8 Thomas Hayles, USA
9 Gert Amentisch, Austria
10 Don Sutton, USA

Veteran men's downhill
1 Walter Brändli, Switzerland
2 Bernard Unhassobiscay, USA
3 Giuseppi Lochi, Italy
4 George Edwards, France
5 Roland Champion, Switzerland
6 Douglas Johnstone, USA
7 Armando Montanari, Italy
8 Tracy Oswell, USA
9 Domenico Elicio, Italy
10 Lorenzo Orlando, Italy

Ruthie Matthes

Every racer's dream – the rainbow jersey. Giovanna Bonazzi celebrates her downhill win in her own country

Men's downhill
1 Francois Gachet, France
2 Tommy Johansson, Sweden
3 Corrado Herin, Italy
4 Tomas Misser, Spain
5 Myles Rockwell, USA
6 Alwx Balaud, France
7 Paolo Caramelino, Italy
8 Greg Herbold, USA
9 Mike King, USA
10 Miles Davies, Austria

Women's downhill
1 Missy Giove, USA
2 Sophie Kempf, France
3 Giovanna Bonazzi, Italy
4 Linda Spiazzi, Italy
5 Rita Burgi, Switzerland
6 Brigitta Kasper, Switzerland
7 Regina Stiefl, Germany
8 Katja Repo, Finland
9 Mikki Douglas, USA
10 Petra Winterhalder, Germany

Junior men's downhill
1 Nicolas Vouilloz, France
2 Pau Misser, Spain
3 Cedric Gracia, France
4 Florent Poussin, France
5 Markus Klausmann, Germany
6 Livio Zampieri, Italy
7 Dario Zampieri, Italy
8 Denis Bonnet, France
9 Alessandro Saligari, Italy
10 Christophe Sauser, Switzerland

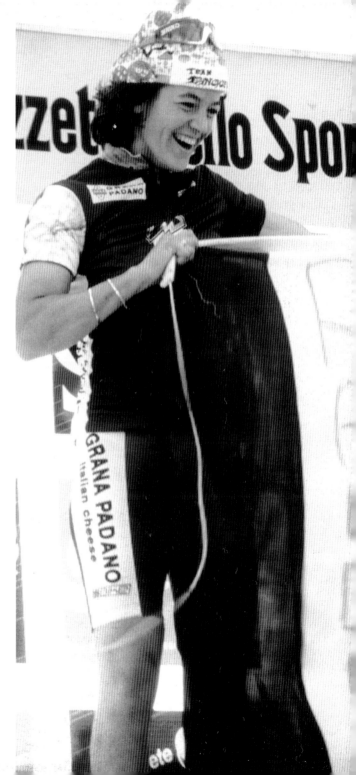

Giovanna Bonazzi

Chantal Daucourt from Switzerland won the European Championships and finished fourth in the World Championships in 1991

Junior women's downhill
1 Anne-Caroline Chausson, France
2 Marielle Saner, Switzerland
3 Mona Fee, France
4 Nolven LeCaer, France
5 Tara Llanes, USA
6 Adriana Santos Nasciemento, Brazil
7 Beth Mozer, USA
8 Melanie Dorian, USA
9 Liane Smidt, South America
10 Nicole Kolb, USA

Veteran men's downhill
1 Walter Brändli, Switzerland
2 Bernard Unhassobiscay, USA
3 Giuseppi Lochi, Italy
4 George Edwards, France
5 Roland Champion, Switzerland
6 Douglas Johnstone, USA
7 Armando Montanari, Italy
8 Tracy Oswell, USA
9 Domenico Elicio, Italy
10 Lorenzo Orlando, Italy

Walter Brändli

1995 Kirchzarten, Germany

Men's cross-country
1 B. Brentjens, Netherlands
2 M. Martinez, France
3 J-E. Ostergaard, Denmark

Women's cross-country
1 A. Sydor, Canada
2 S. Fürst, Switzerland
3 C. Daucourt, Switzerland

Junior men's cross-country
1 T. Kalberer, Switzerland
2 E. Jungaker, Sweden
3 C. Evans, Australia

Junior women's cross-country
1 M. Fee, France
2 K. Hanusova, Czech Rep.
3 C. Potts, USA

Veteran men's cross-country
1 S. Oskwarek, France
2 M. Noris, Italy
3 R. De Bie, Belgium

Veteran women's cross-country
1 C. Waters, USA
2 L. Lamoureaux, USA
3 L. Grassi, Italy

Men's downhill
1 N. Vouilloz, France
2 F. Gachet, France
3 M. King, USA

Women's downhill
1 L. Donovan, USA
2 M. Gonzalez, Spain
3 G. Bonazzi, Italy

Junior men's downhill
1 C. Gracia, France
2 M. Klausmann, Germany
3 F. Poussin, France

Junior women's downhill
1 A-C. Chausson, France
2 N. Le Caer, France
3 M. Saner, Switzerland

Veteran men's downhill
1 E. Barone, France
2 B. Unhassobiscay, USA
3 W. Brändli, Switzerland

The veteran women's downhill event was not contested because riders from only four nations competed in the seeding run. Under UCI rules, at least five nations must take part in world championship level events.

Further reading

The Complete Guide to Sports Nutrition by Anita Bean

A & C Black, 1993

Practical and accessible advice on nutrition for all sportspeople. Eating plans and delicious recipes provided. The definitive sports nutrition book.

Sports Nutrition for Women eds. Anita Bean & Peggy Wellington

A & C Black, 1995

Unique insight into the specific nutritional requirements of active women. Essential reading for all sportswomen.

Flexibility: Principles and Practice by Christopher Norris

A & C Black, 1994

A clearly illustrated guide to stretching by a chartered physiotherapist and sports scientist.

Mountain Bikes Maintenance and Repair by John Stevenson & Brant Richards

Springfield Books/A & C Black, 1992

Guides you expertly through the minefield of everything mechanical on your mountain bike.

The Cyclist's Body Book by Frank Westell & Simon Martin

Springfield Books/A & C Black, 1991

Comprehensive information on training, massage, diet and injuries. Good training section with details of the four levels of training and how to peak for big races.

Advanced Mountain Biking by Derek Purdy

Springfield Books/A & C Black, 1994

If you dream of riding into the wide blue yonder, make sure you've read this book before you go.

A Guide to Cycling Injuries by Dr Dowhnall MacAuley

Springfield Books/A & C Black, 1995

An invaluable source of sound advice on sports medicine at your finger-tips.

Index